STUDENT UNIT GUIDE

A2 Geography

UNIT 6

Edexcel

Specification A

Unit 6

Synoptic: People and Their Environments

Nigel Yates

Philip Allan Updates
Market Place
Deddington
Oxfordshire
OX15 0SE

tel: 01869 338652
fax: 01869 337590
e-mail: sales@philipallan.co.uk
www.philipallan.co.uk

ISBN-13: 978-0-86003-698-2
ISBN-10: 0-86003-698-7

This Guide has been written specifically to support students preparing for the Edexcel Specification A A2 Geography Unit 6 examination. The content has been neither approved nor endorsed by Edexcel and remains the sole responsibility of the author.

Printed by Information Press, Eynsham, Oxford

Environmental information
The paper on which this title is printed is sourced from managed, sustainable forests.

P00496

Contents

Introduction

About this guide

This guide is for students following the Edexcel Specification A A2 Geography course. It aims to guide you through Unit Test 6, which examines the content of **Unit 6: Synoptic: People and Their Environments**.

This guide will clarify:

- the content of the unit so that you know and understand what you have to learn
- the nature of the unit test
- the geographical skills and techniques that you will need to know for the assessment
- the standards you will need to reach to achieve a particular grade
- the examination techniques you will require to improve your performance and maximise your achievement

This **Introduction** reviews the main features of the unit and the approaches to studying it. Some of the techniques commonly used in writing good essays are also explained, with coverage of command words and some advice on how to construct examination answers.

The **Content Guidance** section summarises the essential material for Unit 6. The aim is to make you aware of the type of information and understanding of abstract concepts that you will need to make sense of the facts.

The **Question and Answer** section presents essays drawn from each section of the unit. Each answer includes a detailed analysis from a senior examiner, illustrating both the positive and the negative aspects of the essay.

A2 Geography

The A2 course is designed for those who have already completed AS Geography. It has different units from the AS course and is intended to be more demanding. The course will enable you to combine your AS results with your A2 results to receive an A-level grade.

Scheme of assessment

Unit 6: Synoptic: People and Their Environments is one of three units that make up the A2 specification. The A2 element is worth 50% of the full A-level qualification. In this specification, there are no options as to which units you can study; all candidates must take Units 4, 5 and 6.

The Unit 6 test is marked out of 75, but you are awarded a uniform mark for the paper, which is out of 120. Although you are not awarded a grade for each unit, the marks awarded are equivalent to the following grades: 96–120 = A; 84–95 = B; 72–83 = C; 60–71 = D; 48–59 = E; < 48 = U.

Unit	Unit test length	Max. mark	Max. uniform mark	A2 weighting
4: Physical Systems, Processes and Patterns	1 hour 30 minutes	50	90	30%
5: Human Systems, Processes and Patterns	1 hour 30 minutes	50	90	30%
6: Synoptic	2 hours	75	120	40%

Unit 6

- There are 24 synoptic links, two for each section of Units 1, 2, 4 and 5 (each unit has three sections).
- The synoptic paper contains five questions.
- Question 1 is divided into four subsections. It is *compulsory* and worth 50 marks.
- Questions 2, 3, 4 and 5 are essay questions, each corresponding to a synoptic theme and worth 25 marks. You choose *one* of these to answer.

Question 1

Question 1 involves responding to previously unseen resources, generally including a map, text, graphs, photographs and diagrams. This question tests your ability to interpret these resources and to apply your geographical understanding and skills to the material.

Typical questions are:

- With reference to...assess the impact of the physical environment on settlement and population in...
- Using the map and item...examine the impact of human activity on the physical environment in...
- With reference to...evaluate the success of the management of the...
- In what ways can economic development be regarded as sustainable in...

These questions are drawn from the four synoptic themes but do *not* assume detailed knowledge of each theme. They *do* assume a broad understanding of the key ideas and terminology.

Question 1 is worth 50 out of 75 marks and should occupy two-thirds of your allotted time — 80 out of 120 minutes. This one question carries 80 uniform marks towards your final A-level result — almost as many as the 90 uniform marks carried by the Unit 4 and Unit 5 tests.

Skills to practise for Question 1

- Annotation — do this as you read through the resource booklet, making comments and underlining or highlighting text that might be useful, and annotating photographs by explaining features rather than simply describing them.
- Description of trends in data — try to spot general trends (up/down/variable) and then pick out anomalies or obvious inconsistencies.
- Description of patterns or distributions on maps — try to spot general patterns (even/uneven) and then pick out anomalies or obvious inconsistencies.
- Drawing sketch maps — you may not be asked to do this as an examination task, but a well-annotated sketch map is often a very economical way of answering a question. If you draw sketch maps, make sure that you refer to them in your answers.

The essay question

You are required to answer one of the four essay titles. Each title is drawn from a synoptic theme:

- Question 2: Physical environments influence human activity (synoptic theme 6.1)
- Question 3: Human activities modify physical environments (synoptic theme 6.2)
- Question 4: Physical and human resources may be exploited, managed and protected (synoptic theme 6.3)
- Question 5: Communities and their governance influence geographical inter-relationships at a range of scales (synoptic theme 6.4)

The essays require a *full understanding* and *knowledge* of the synoptic links that feed into these themes. The titles will allow you to draw on knowledge from several links and will not ask for any particular process or any particular environment. Hence, titles will not be as vague as 'Assess the impact of the physical environment on man' or as precise as 'Assess the impact of hurricanes on the economy and environment of LEDCs'. They will be somewhere in between, as in 'Compare the short-term and long-term impact of hazards on human activity'.

As you only have to answer one essay question, it is likely that you have been taught the synoptic links that relate specifically to one or two of these possible titles, rather than all four. The links can be grouped by theme, although some fall into more than one category.

Theme 1: Physical environments influence human activity

- Positive and negative impacts of earthquakes and volcanoes on human activity, both short term and long term
- The reasons for, and methods of, groundwater and river management in countries at different states of development
- The need for coastal management schemes
- Weather hazards and their impact on human activity, to include hurricanes, tornadoes and drought, with an emphasis on recent events
- Opportunities and challenges exist in upland areas (either glaciated in the past

and/or currently active) for tourism, energy production, quarrying, transport, agriculture, settlement etc.

- Periglacial and permafrost environments present their own challenges and opportunities

Theme 2: Human activities modify physical environments

- The reasons for, and methods of, groundwater and river management in countries at different states of development
- The causes and consequences of recent migrations and refugee movements
- Possible impacts of humans on weather and climate — including pollution, ozone destruction, global warming and cloud seeding
- The causes and management of soil erosion
- The interrelationships between the physical environment and industrial location, and the management of environmental impact
- The growth of the leisure and tourist industry, and its social, cultural and economic impact on rural environments

Theme 3: Physical and human resources may be exploited, managed and protected

- The importance of risk assessment, prediction and monitoring, and their limitations
- Decision-making issues related to the management of the hydrological cycle
- Issues of management, including methods and strategies used, and their possible impact
- The management opportunities and challenges associated with grassland and forest ecosystems
- The causes and management of soil erosion
- The management of waste in cities — the problems of water and air quality control, and waste disposal
- The concept of sustainable and unsustainable development at national and global scales

Theme 4: Communities and their governance influence geographical interrelationships at a range of scales

- Data collection (e.g. census) and its role in planning and providing services for a changing population
- Government policies to increase and reduce birth rates — reasons, effects and relative success
- Policies for managing changing rural and urban settlement
- Issues, rationales and outcomes of policies
- Reasons for, effects of, and issues associated with government policies to influence migration into, out of, and within a country
- The role of government in the control and modification of the relationship between industry and the environment, and the response to changing values and attitudes within society as a whole
- The role of values and attitudes in determining the type and rate of development

Revision advice

You should keep your synoptic notes in a separate folder or section of your folder. Organisation is critical here because you will have been taught the 'links' at different stages of the course, possibly by different teachers.

It is important that you keep up to date with your studying and complete all work set on time. If you are absent for any reason, you need to find out what you missed and catch up as quickly as possible. Hopefully, you will have some time for revision at the end of the course and you should try to make full use of any opportunities that you are given.

When you are revising on your own, try to do the following:

- Plan a revision schedule that gives fairly even time allocation to each of your subjects and to each unit within the subject.
- Stick to the schedule!
- Read through all material relating to a topic — notes, handouts, questions, worksheets, etc.
- Make revision notes that summarise the key elements of the topic (the Content Guidance section of this book will help).
- Make a list of the key facts/figures for each of the main case studies/examples that you need.
- Practise sample/past examination questions (such as the ones in the Question and Answer section).
- Ask your teacher/lecturer to clarify any topics/issues about which you are uncertain.
- Remember, you need to revise *all* of the specification content in this unit.

Examination skills

Understanding the question

Students often achieve a low mark in an examination essay because they have not fully understood the question. To score high marks you need to understand how the question should be answered. It helps if you analyse the question and identify its components and command words.

Components of a question

Most essay titles or examination questions contain the following components:

- subject matter or topic — what, in general terms, is the question about? From what section of the specification is it drawn?
- aspect or focus — this is the angle or point of view on the subject matter. What aspect of the subject matter is the question about?
- command or instruction — this refers to the command word or phrase which tells the student exactly what to do.
- restriction or expansion of the subject matter — this is the detailed limitation of the topic. What, in specific terms, is the question about? Is it all industry or just manufacturing industry?

- viewpoint — you may be required to write from a viewpoint dictated by the question. Such a question could begin with 'Criticise the view that...'

Command words

Exam questions use a series of command words that you need to understand. The list below explains the meaning of the commonly used command words.

- **Account for:** give the reasons for the subject of the question.
- **Analyse:** take apart an idea, concept or statement, in order to consider all the factors of which it consists. Answers of this type should be very methodical and logically organised.
- **Assess the view that:** explore a point of view and deliver a judgement as to the validity of that view.
- **Compare:** set items side by side and show their similarities and differences. A balanced, objective answer is expected.
- **Consider:** describe and give your thoughts on the subject.
- **Contrast:** point out only the differences between two items.
- **Criticise:** point out mistakes or weaknesses, but *also* indicate any favourable aspects of the subject of the question.
- **Critically examine the view that:** explore a point of view from both a positive and negative perspective, offering evidence and delivering a judgement.
- **Define:** explain the precise meaning of a concept. This should include recognition of any difficulties in defining the term.
- **Describe:** say what something is like, how it works and so on.
- **Discuss:** explain an item or concept, and then give details about it, using supportive information, examples, points for and against, and explanations for the facts put forward. It is important to give both sides of an argument and come to a conclusion.
- **Distinguish between:** define two or more concepts and point out the differences between them using comparative language such as 'less', 'more', 'smaller' and 'larger'.
- **Elucidate:** explain what something means and make it clear (lucid).
- **Evaluate/assess:** decide and explain how great, valuable or important something is. The judgement should be backed by a discussion of the evidence or reasoning involved.
- **Examine:** investigate in detail, offering evidence both for and against a point of view or a judgement. Both description and explanation are likely to be required, and some sort of personal observations or comments are expected.
- **Explain:** offer a detailed and exact explanation of an idea or principle, or a set of reasons for a situation or attitude.
- **Explore:** examine the subject thoroughly and consider it from a variety of viewpoints.
- **Illustrate:** provide examples to demonstrate or prove the subject of the question. This command is often added to another instruction.
- **Justify:** give only the reasons for a position or argument, and the main objections likely to be made to them.

- **State:** express the relevant points briefly and clearly, without lengthy discussion or minor details.
- **Summarise/outline:** provide a summary of all the available information about a subject. Questions of this type often require short answers.
- **Trace:** state and describe briefly, in logical or chronological order, the stages in the development of a theory, a settlement pattern, a process, etc.
- **To what extent is it true that...:** discuss and explain in what ways the statement is true and in what ways it is not true.

Analysing the question

- Identify the **topic** (put a circle around it).
- Recognise the **command** (underline it).
- Search for the **aspect** — this is the angle or point of view on the subject matter.
- If the topic has a **restriction** or **expansion**, identify it.

Answering the question

How to produce quality responses to Question 1

Before beginning your answer to Question 1, you should:

- read the subsections to get a general idea of the tasks required
- ring or highlight key command words. If necessary, deconstruct the questions. Watch out for any obvious restrictions.
- look at the mark allocation so that you can recognise the *really* important sections. Note down the time that you should be spending on your answer. This works out at approximately 1.5 minutes per mark. Therefore, a section worth 16 marks should take you about 24 minutes to complete, including time to read and absorb the relevant resources.
- read the text sections and highlight and/or scribble comments about them. Pay particular attention to the introduction, which often contains very useful general information. Make comments that extend from the text.

When answering Question 1 you should:

- use all of the material — it is all there for a reason, so when you have finished, check that each resource item has been used in some way.
- try to use your own words — don't lift great chunks of text if you can avoid it. For every piece of text that you use, make a comment about how it relates to the question asked. Be explicit.
- obey the command words and phrases absolutely. Never do more than they ask you to do and try not to do less. The hardest thing to do is to resist the temptation to explain, when only asked to describe. You won't lose marks, but you will have wasted your time.

In order to trigger higher bands in the mark scheme, try to:

- make links between different resources and cross-reference when you do so. For instance, 'as Item 3 suggests, the pattern of land use shown in Item 1 might be explained by...'

- apply understanding of processes from other parts of the specification. Be explicit.
- apply knowledge of other areas that you have studied. It is perfectly legitimate to draw contrasts with other regions or areas that you have covered. However, you must be careful not to stray from the question asked. For example, in answering the question, 'Examine the possible impact of the Three Gorges project on...' you could compare this project with other large dam schemes and apply understanding of the processes that are associated with the hydrological changes that dams cause.
- use words like 'therefore' and 'however' to qualify your comments.
- look at the mark allocation and time yourself carefully. Don't neglect the long last section because of shortage of time.

Typical features of a top-level answer include:

- wide-ranging and accurate knowledge
- thorough explanation and balanced discussion of all dimensions of the question
- an understanding of the concepts and the use of these to support the argument
- detailed examples, with a range of diagrams, maps and data used appropriately
- comparisons of scale, in space and time, to support the discussion
- fluent English, expressing complex ideas clearly and with few errors in grammar, punctuation and spelling

Writing an essay plan

You will have written essay plans while preparing for the examination and as a part of your course.

- Begin by highlighting or circling the key words in the title.
- Outline the key themes that you would like to address, under separate headings.
- Look very carefully at the resource, noting anything that might be useful in the construction of your answer.
- Refer to it in your answer should it seem appropriate to do so.

You should not spend more than 4 or 5 minutes doing this.

The introduction to the essay

The introduction should be a context statement, which says something meaningful. Clarify your terms by extending definitions or point out how some of the terms used in the question are difficult or problematic. Try to set the tone of the essay by stating how this topic interrelates with others.

The middle (analytical part) of the essay

The core of the essay should be organised in paragraphs, each of which takes on an aspect of the question, with examples. Structure it logically by tackling one point in each paragraph. Do not drift off into themes or evidence that are not what the question requires. Use evidence constructively and make it work for you. Remember that you can never lose marks. A bold guess is better than nothing. You may have only a hazy recall of the precise rate at which the Amazonian rainforest decreased in the 1980s, but better a hazy idea than none at all. If in doubt, include it!

Each paragraph should be constructed as follows:

- Make a point.
- Offer an example or evidence to support that point.
- Offer a comment that ties that point to the question set.

In your analysis of the question, bear in mind the following:

- **contrasts in scale** — does your answer tackle the fact that some explanations work at some scales but not at others? Hence, climate might be the key variable in controlling agricultural land use at a global scale but not at a local scale.
- **contrasts in space** — does your answer allow for the fact that what is true for one part of the world may not apply to another? An example of this is the contrast between MEDCs and LEDCs.
- **contrasts in time** — does your answer allow for the fact that explanations will vary from one period to another? What was true in 1945 may not be true today. For example, a theory such as Weber's may well be applicable in the circumstances of one period, but not another.

The end (conclusion) of the essay

This should *not* be a précis of the middle part. Start your conclusions by referring back to the original question and its key aspects or proposition. Try to leave the examiner with the impression that you could have said more if only you had been allowed the time. All conclusions in human geography are liable to be partial, tentative and incomplete, and you are perfectly entitled to say so.

Content Guidance

There are four sections in the specification content for Unit 6:

(1) Physical environments influence human activity

(2) Human activities modify physical environments

(3) Physical and human resources may be exploited, managed and protected

(4) Communities and their governance influence geographical interrelationships at a range of scales

In this Content Guidance, each of the four elements is considered in terms of:

- the key concepts involved
- the content required
- the use of examples and case studies

This should make it clear to you what you need to know and understand.

Synoptic links from Unit 1

Relationships between people and tectonic environments

Exam tip There is a sequence of useful pairs you can use while analysing the impact of hazards on human activity:

- positive and negative
- short term and long term
- human and economic
- small scale and large scale (micro- and macro-)
- MEDCs and LEDCs

The impacts of earthquakes

Ground displacement

Ground displacement itself is not life threatening. However, the impact of ground movements on buildings and structures, such as bridges and roads, is. The worst earthquake catastrophe in an MEDC for many years, the Kobe earthquake, occurred on western Honshu Island in Japan in 1995. More than 5000 people perished in southern Hyogo prefecture, most in the city of Kobe, Japan's most important port. Surface rupture of the fault was observed only in a rural area of Awaji Island, where there were displacements of up to 3 metres. Few structures were near enough the fault to be damaged by this displacement, although underground utilities, fences and irrigation ditches were cut. The loss of so many lives, in a country where so much effort had been made to prepare for earthquakes, shocked observers worldwide. Many earthquake faults never break the surface, ruling out direct effects.

Landslides

Landslides are movements of a mass of rock, earth or debris down a slope. Such slope failures can be triggered by a number of events including earthquakes. One of the best-documented landslides occurred on Mt St Helens in 1980 when an earthquake of magnitude 5.0 triggered a rapid series of events. The northern slope of the mountain failed and began to slide downwards. This huge landslide released a tremendous mass from above a hydrothermal system that had driven earlier steam eruptions. The sudden loss of confining pressure above the heated groundwater caused a massive hydrothermal blast that was directed sideways through the landslide scarp.

Liquefaction

Liquefaction of loose, water-saturated sands and other granular soils due to earthquake shaking is a major cause of damage to, and destruction of, constructed facilities. Such soils amplify the seismic waves and firm ground becomes soft — liquefaction. One of the major impacts of liquefaction-induced ground failure is sideways spreading of sloping ground.

The 1985 earthquake centred beneath Mexico City occurred when the Cocos plate lying beneath the Pacific Ocean broke free from the North American plate. The power of this magnitude 8.1 earthquake was great. When the shaking stopped, 18 million people in Mexico City began assessing damage. Thousands lay buried. In the Benito Jaurez Hospital alone, over 1000 people died. A shift change of staff was taking place just as the hospital collapsed.

The Mexico City earthquake occurred as two separate events 26 seconds apart. The city lies on the remains of an ancient lakebed — an unstable subsoil of sand, mud on top of clay, and gravel, all held in a shallow geological saucer of bedrock. This mixture is so soft that even in normal conditions, buildings in Mexico City can sink a few centimetres every year. During the earthquake, buildings swayed for over 3 minutes as the ground liquefied.

Mexico City lies over the remains of the Aztec capital, Tenochtitlan. Excellent construction techniques used by the Aztecs were demonstrated during the earthquake. Both the Metropolitan Cathedral (built by the Aztecs in 1525) and the National Palace (built around 1700) remained standing, whereas modern buildings on the same block collapsed.

Tsunamis

Tsunamis are waves with extremely long wavelengths that travel across the ocean. They are usually created by volcanic activity or landslides. The tsunami that struck New Guinea in 1998 was the most devastating for many years. The magnitude of the earthquake that triggered it was 7.1, and the epicentre was in northern New Guinea near the coast. It generated waves 7–10 metres high which, it is estimated, killed 4000 people who were crushed, maimed or pulled out to sea and drowned as the waves withdrew. At least seven villages were obliterated. Many of the dead were children, who had no chance of battling the phenomenally powerful waves.

New Guinea is a seismically active region, the site of an island arc–continent collision, where tectonic plates are converging and sliding past each other.

Fires

In the San Francisco earthquake of 1906, fire was the main cause of lost property, as it was in San Francisco in 1989, in Northridge, California in 1994 and in Kobe in 1995. In 1906, this was unavoidable — fire protection was in its infancy. In the more recent earthquakes, the largest fires started primarily as a result of ruptured gas lines and fallen power lines. Fire protection is expensive and requires continual expenditure to maintain the necessary equipment and workforce. The costs of providing full cover to a city are prohibitive, given that the number of machines and personnel likely to be needed to cover a major earthquake far exceeds 'normal' daily requirements. This raises significant issues about the costs and benefits of such life-saving systems.

Exam tip

- None of these physical events can be regarded as positive unless they cause the destruction of a human environment that is regarded as deeply unattractive, therefore giving an opportunity for urban renewal.
- The destruction caused by the Kobe earthquake is a useful reminder that MEDCs are not immune from heavy loss of life, despite the contrast between the human and economic costs of hazards in MEDCs and LEDCs.

- The Mexico City earthquake effectively illustrates how significant time of day can be in determining fatalities and how the ground conditions are critical. It also reinforces a point that could be made about Kobe — despite our modern assumption of superior technology, we are still vulnerable.
- If you use Mt St Helens as a case study, it is a good idea to add a new dimension. One way would be to use it to illustrate how hazards are multifaceted. In the Mt St Helens eruption this is shown by the sequence of events — earthquake, landslide, steam (phreatic) eruption, followed by volcanic eruption. It would also be worth pointing out how floods, mudslides and gas clouds were responsible for almost all the loss of life.

The impacts of volcanoes

Volcanic hazards are complicated by the fact that volcanic areas are often attractive to settlement, thus increasing the number of people likely to be affected. The reasons why these areas are attractive might include:

- **minerals and natural resources** — volcanoes bring to the surface of the Earth many valuable resources, such as diamonds, copper and gold. For example, ancient deposits found in association with volcanoes are some of the most important sources of gold in Canada. Obsidian (volcanic glass) was the hardest substance known to Palaeolithic man and much prized. Ancient seafloor volcanoes contributed to massive accumulations of base metals such as lead, zinc and copper. In a longer time frame, volcanoes are responsible for most of the water on the surface of the Earth — hence they might be considered necessary for life.
- **fertile soils** — volcanoes provide nutrients to the surrounding soil. Volcanic ash often contains minerals beneficial to plants and if it is very fine ash, it breaks down quickly and becomes mixed into the soil. Areas that benefit include Indonesia, the Philippines, Japan and parts of Italy. A good example is Java in Indonesia, with its very high-density rural population based on wet-rice agriculture, which has thrived for millennia in the volcanic soils of the island.
- **hydrothermal energy** — Iceland is located on the north mid-Atlantic ridge and is crossed by an active volcanic zone going from southwest to northeast that is an enormous potential source of thermal energy. Water running through the Earth's crust brings this geothermal energy to the surface, where it emerges in hot springs and **fumaroles**. There are hot springs all over the country. They are classified as high- or low-temperature springs, depending on whether the temperature is above or below 150°C. In Iceland, geothermal energy is used extensively for space heating, electricity generation and industrial applications. The exploitation of this resource is largely responsible for the growth, over the last 100 years, of the capital, Reykjavik. It is a good example of turning a potential hazard into something useful.
- **tourism** — in modern Western cultures, volcanoes are seen as being both beautiful and threatening. In many MEDCs, volcanic regions (both active and extinct) generate considerable interest from visitors. This is exploited by local authorities wishing to generate employment in what are frequently quite remote regions. Examples include Iceland, which has capitalised on its tectonic activity in recent years in an attempt to diversify its economy. Organised trips to the many volcanoes

of Hawaii, to Mt St Helens or to the geysers of Yellowstone National Park are critical to the economy of these areas.

Exam tip Unlike earthquakes, volcanoes can be said to have a positive impact. This positive impact can be treated as both very long term (e.g. the creation of water) and medium term (e.g. the creation of fertile soils). The costs (losses) are almost all short term.

Volcanoes as hazards

Volcanic hazards vary with the nature of the magma. **Acidic magma** (>66% silica content) produces *explosive* volcanic action where the main risks are from **pyroclastic flows** (also known as *nuée ardente*), **ash** and **lahars**. **Basic magma** (45–52% silica) produces effusive volcanic action with the main risks being from ash and lava flows. There is a **magnitude–frequency** relationship with volcanoes — larger eruptions occur less often. Sometimes the structure and the chemistry of a volcano are more complicated and so the volcano does not fit expectations. For example, Mt Vesuvius, which is on a destructive boundary, has acidic explosive magma — as one would expect — but nearby Stromboli has relatively basic magma, coming from a deeper source nearer the mantle.

A volcanic **hazard** refers to any potentially dangerous volcanic occurrence. A volcanic **risk** is any potential loss or damage as a result of the hazard that might be incurred by people and property, or which impacts negatively on the productive capacity or sustainability of a population. Risk not only includes the potential monetary and human losses, but also a population's vulnerability.

Volcanoes may be associated with a range of related hazards, including:

- pyroclastic flows (e.g. Mt Pelée)
- lahars (e.g. Nevada del Ruis)
- ashfall (e.g. Hekla)
- lava flows (e.g. Heimay)
- torrential rain and floods (e.g. Pinatubo)
- earthquakes and tsunami (e.g. Krakatoa)
- gas asphyxiation (Lake Nyos, Cameroon)
- jökulhlaup — a sudden release of glacial water (Vatnajökull, Iceland)

It was estimated that 500 million people would be at risk from volcanic hazards by the year 2000. In the past 500 years, over 200 000 people have lost their lives because of volcanic eruptions. In recent years, there have been about 1000 deaths per year, which is far greater than the death rate for previous centuries. The reason for this increase is not increased volcanism, but because more people are populating the flanks of active volcanoes and valley areas near those volcanoes.

The human impact of earthquakes and volcanic activity

The human impact of earthquakes and volcanic activity is dependent upon:

- the severity of the event and its duration
- the population density of the affected region
- the preparedness of the population

In common with all other hazards, this involves both **human costs** and **economic costs**. These are related in that loss of life, as well as having social and psychological impacts, has a profound economic impact.

Human costs

These can be sub-divided into:

- **primary casualties** — people who are killed or injured directly as a result of the earthquake (by fire, structural collapse or other physical hazards related to the shaking). Their numbers tend to be much higher in LEDCs than in MEDCs, because of poor construction methods.
- **secondary casualties** — people who survive the initial incident, are injured during the process, and die because of inadequate resources and the inability to access effective and immediate emergency medical care. Numbers tend to be higher in LEDCs than MEDCs, because of limited resources.
- **tertiary casualties** — people who suffer from pre-existing medical conditions that are aggravated by the earthquake. This group also includes those who become sick and may die as a result of the post-disaster environment, largely through infectious diseases. In LEDCs, this is very often the largest group of casualties.

The death tolls resulting from some volcanic eruptions and earthquakes are shown in the following tables:

Year	Volcanic eruption	Death toll
79	Vesuvius, Italy	16 000
1815	Tambora, Indonesia	92 000
1985	Nevado del Ruiz, Colombia	23 000
1980	Mt St Helens, USA	57

Year	Site of earthquake	Death toll
1556	Shen-Shu, China	830 000
1783	Calabria, Italy	50 000
1906	San Francisco, USA	700
1989	Loma Prieta, USA	40
1999	Turkey	15 000

Economic costs

Indirect costs include the immediate costs of repairing damage caused by the event. For example, the estimated repair costs for the Kobe earthquake ranged from \$95 billion to \$147 billion. **Indirect costs** include the loss of earnings caused by the disaster. If the disruption is prolonged and the infrastructure is complex, then these can run into billions of dollars. Increasingly, major natural hazards are causing secondary technological and industrial accidents and emergencies. After the recent earthquake in Turkey, a major refinery fire greatly reduced capacity for the entire country, which threatened the safety and health of earthquake victims. These costs may run on for many years and are difficult to evaluate accurately.

Exam tip The human and economic impact of volcanic eruptions is rising, largely because there are more people and we are better insured. The frequency of the events is probably no greater now than it was a century ago. Hazards only become disasters when we 'get in the way'. The 'costs' of loss of life and bereavement are calculated for insurance purposes using a formula that, among other things, multiplies earning potential by life expectancy. You could make this point about the 'costs' of hazards to illustrate the inherent problems of such calculations.

Risk assessment

Earthquakes

Earthquake records suggest that there is an increasing number of earthquakes that cause higher levels of destruction. This is because human populations have expanded into earthquake-risk zones and man-made structures are increasingly expensive and vulnerable. Since earthquakes have a frequency–magnitude relationship, some areas which have infrequent but violent earthquakes have been colonised with little awareness of the potential danger. The eastern seaboard of the USA is an example.

Where written records of earthquakes do not exist, it is possible to use geological and soil maps to identify clues to past earthquake activity. Once the geological record is understood, areas of particular risk can be mapped. Areas of high risk include steep slopes, sensitive soils and low-lying coastal areas. Risk assessment also has to take into account the nature of the settlement and the infrastructure — medium-height buildings are more vulnerable than either tall or low buildings. Masonry buildings are more vulnerable than wooden or steel-framed buildings, but wooden buildings are more prone to fire risk. The location of mains services (electricity, water or gas) may have an impact on potential damage. The size and design of roads and bridges will have considerable impact on evacuation, emergency access and potential loss of life.

Volcanoes

Volcanic risk assessment includes:

- monitoring current levels of activity
- mapping evidence for destruction in previous eruptions

While it is feasible to modify lava flows by damming, cooling (with water) and bombing, the only realistic approach to living with volcanoes is avoiding high-risk sites (e.g. mudflow tracks) and evacuating as necessary. The recent history of human settlement on the slopes of Vesuvius shows that avoidance of high-risk areas is a strategy that is widely ignored.

Prediction and monitoring

Earthquake prediction

While there are many potential indicators for earthquakes, none has proved reliable. Key areas of research and monitoring include:

- P-wave/S-wave ratio — this ratio drops before a large earthquake
- warning activity — there is an increase in the number of small earth tremors (**foreshocks**) before a major shock
- water levels in wells — these rise or fall as the rocks are squeezed by the increasing strain before an earthquake
- radon gas levels in wells — this radioactive gas is squeezed out from rock pores by the build up of strain
- changes in the electrical properties of rock — increasing strain causes rearrangement of the crystal structures (in extreme cases, this produces light displays — the so-called 'earthquake lights' phenomenon)
- ground deformation — this occurs as rocks are strained; it can be surveyed on the ground using laser-ranging techniques or can be measured by accurate radar imagery from satellites
- unusual behaviour in animals before earthquakes — we could either monitor animal behaviour or identify and monitor the sensory cues they use (e.g. subsonic vibrations, magnetism or electrical sensitivity)

Some earthquakes have been predicted but most have come with no obvious warning. Hence, there is public mistrust of the reliability of prediction.

Monitoring volcanoes

An eruption takes place when the pressure of upwelling magma is no longer balanced by the weight and rigidity of the overlying rocks. Since these rocks are riddled with fractures and inconsistencies, it is difficult to predict *whether, when* or *where* an eruption will take place. However, volcanoes are monitored to try to predict eruptions. The methods include:

- **inflation monitoring** — this checks the bulging of the volcano as magma approaches the surface
- **gas sampling** — changes in gas composition reflect activity levels in the magma underground
- **geothermal monitoring** from space — this registers changes in heat flow as magma approaches the surface
- **seismic monitoring** — this 'listens' to the rising blobs of magma as they force their way upwards

The main difficulties in predicting volcanic activity are that:

- magma may be generated from different depths and arrive at the surface by different routes
- the nature and chemistry of the magma change over time and may be different from one phase of a volcano's life to another

Planning for earthquakes

The most logical assumption to make when planning for an earthquake is that everything will be destroyed. This is because it is better to plan to have *nothing* available than to depend on things that might not be functioning. Even a moderate earthquake of magnitude 6.0 is enough to damage many structures and disrupt life severely.

The impact of an earthquake of magnitude 8.3 occurring near a major population centre has been predicted as follows:

- Severe damage will be widespread, perhaps ranging hundreds of kilometres. Moderate damage could occur up to 300 kilometres from the epicentre.
- Surface waves produced by subduction zone earthquakes can last for several minutes, accentuating the effects of soil liquefaction, which may cause extensive structural collapse, particularly of tall buildings.
- Infrastructure (communications, utilities, transportation systems) may be disrupted for at least 24 hours, perhaps longer.
- Landslides will occur in areas with significant slope hazard.
- Tsunamis will be generated, resulting in major damage both locally and at distant sites, frequently without any warning.
- Injuries and death will occur as a result of structural collapse, and some of the collapses will be buildings of critical importance, such as hospitals, emergency operations and communication centres. While many buildings are strengthened against earthquakes, few are capable of withstanding a magnitude 8 earthquake. Many homes will be destroyed, although newer structures (wood-frame, rectangular footprint) may survive with moderate damage.

Regardless of the severity of the earthquake, several factors are probably valid:

- Earthquakes occur without warning, and pre-event response activity will not be possible.
- The probability of the event occurring during non-working hours is greater than 3:1.
- Damage to sensitive communications systems will interfere with response management.
- Aftershocks are likely, causing additional damage, interfering with response efforts and causing unease among the population.

Exam tip The main problem with planning for disasters is that they cannot be anticipated. It has been estimated that there is a 1 in 20 chance that a major earthquake will strike southern California in the next 50 years. However, this probability is essentially meaningless because it is based on past averages, rather than on measurement of the causal factors.

Earthquakes are unpredictable and occur with no warning, so the risk is imprecise. People are not easily excited by non-specific risks without precise dates attached. We are reluctant to think about things that *may* kill or injure us, or our loved ones.

Emergency planning is very expensive and, with virtually no return on investment, it is difficult to encourage spending on preparedness and equipment. Although the choice is one of 'pay now, or pay big later', it is often not seen in that light. Politicians and citizens, more concerned with short-term problems, do not see the potential threat as a major concern. There are very few votes to be had in raising taxes to pay for improvements in, for example, a fire-service that may not be needed in one's lifetime.

The hydrological cycle is used and managed

Reasons for the management of water resources include the following:

- Water is essential for drinking, crop irrigation and the provision of power.
- There is frequent competition between water consumers, both within and between nations.
- Growing populations in many LEDCs pose problems for future demand.
- Population movements in some MEDCs (e.g. USA) have altered the pattern of demand within those countries.

Issues of *quantity* and *quality* of this essential resource dominate water management.

Groundwater

Groundwater is water that occurs underground in gaps and spaces in soil, sand and rocks. The area where water fills these spaces is called the **saturated zone**, the top of which is the **water table**. The water table may be only a few centimetres below the ground surface, or hundreds of metres down.

Groundwater occurs almost everywhere, even in arid regions. The water table may be deep or near the surface and may rise or fall, both seasonally and in the longer term. Heavy rain or melting snow may cause the water table to rise; an extended period of dry weather may cause it to fall. Groundwater moves slowly through layers of soil, sand and rocks which are known as **aquifers**. The speed of flow depends on the size of the spaces in the soil or rock and how well the spaces are connected. Aquifers typically consist of gravel, sand, sandstone or fractured rock, such as limestone. Water in aquifers may be brought to the surface naturally through a spring or by being discharged into lakes and streams. It can also be extracted by a **well** drilled into the aquifer and brought to the surface using a pump. **Artesian wells** rely on natural pressure to force the water up and out of the well.

In some areas, people face serious water shortages because groundwater is being used more rapidly than it is replenished; in other areas, groundwater may be polluted from landfill, septic tanks, leaky underground gas tanks or from overuse of fertilisers and pesticides. Pollution occurs if the material above the aquifer is permeable, allowing pollutants to sink into the groundwater.

Water supply and quality in an MEDC

In many MEDCs, the issue of water contamination is at least as important as that of water supply. Groundwater contaminants in Michigan, USA, are shown below:

Organic chemicals	Inorganic substances	Others
• Industrial solvents (e.g. trichlorethylene, vinyl chloride) • Petroleum products (e.g. benzene, gasoline) • Pesticides	• Nitrates • Fluorides • Arsenic • Brine/salt • Sulphates • Chlorides	• Metals • Radioactive materials (some occurring naturally) • Bacteria

In the last 50 years, the southwest of the USA has experienced rapid population growth, largely through in-migration. Much of this region is arid, with precipitation of less than 300 mm per year. Therefore, one of the most serious issues facing the region is the availability, use and quality of groundwater.

In large sections of the western USA, groundwater is the only dependable source of water for agriculture and domestic consumption. However, many aquifers are being depleted so quickly that they will be dry within a century. The Ogallala aquifer underlies approximately 582 525 km^2 in the Great Plains region, particularly in the high plains of Texas, New Mexico, Oklahoma, Kansas, Colorado and Nebraska (see Figure 1). The depth of the aquifer from the surface varies from region to region.

Figure 1 Location of the Ogallala aquifer

Use of the aquifer began at the turn of the century. Since the Second World War, reliance on it has increased with the rising population. Groundwater withdrawal has now surpassed the aquifer's rate of natural recharge. Some places overlying the aquifer have already exhausted their underground supply. Other parts have more favourable saturated thickness and recharge rates, and so are less vulnerable.

Dependence upon groundwater will increase in many areas. This dependence is already having serious consequences for small towns on the Great Plains. Faced with increasing costs associated with deeper wells and the need for ever more advanced technology for extracting water, these towns lack the resources to maintain current agricultural practices.

Water supply and quality in an LEDC

Groundwater is a vital source of domestic water supply in most LEDCs. In India, roughly 80% of the rural water supply for domestic use comes from groundwater. The presence of wells in villages and towns means that people (particularly women who do most of the agricultural work) do not have to make long daily walks to fetch water from springs or rivers. This frees time and labour for other, more productive, activities. Furthermore, since water is readily available, more is used, which can have major health benefits. In addition, because of filtration by the soil and the long time spent underground, groundwater is usually cleaner than surface sources.

Access to groundwater is a key resource for economic development. In areas dependent on irrigated agriculture, the reliability of groundwater sources and the resulting high crop yields often enable farmers with small landholdings to increase their income. In India, small and marginal farmers (those having less than 2 hectares) own 29% of the agricultural area. However, their share in the net area irrigated by wells is 38.1% and they account for 35.3% of the tube wells fitted with electric pump sets.

Exam tip In arid regions of the world, both in MEDCs and LEDCs, the issue of groundwater management has a growing significance. Until the last 20 years, neglect of this resource has been almost universal. Only now is the rate of groundwater depletion being recognised.

River management

Irrigation

Rivers have provided water for irrigation for at least 6000 years. Even today, in an era of piped water, the alluvial floodplains of the world are the main centres of human population and activity. The complex irrigation systems of Chinese and Indian agriculture gave rise to well-organised states and empires with sophisticated management systems, long before Europeans evolved nation states. China's irrigated areas have increased from 27 million hectares in 1957 to about 51 Mha today — 54% of the total cultivated area. The goal is to bring a further 20 Mha under irrigation, half in new areas and half by increasing efficiency in existing areas. However, water availability is a limiting factor. Overexploitation of groundwater sources and growing competition for surface water, particularly in the north China Plain, are major challenges. About 20% of irrigated areas have waterlogging or soil salinity to varying degrees.

Flood management

Historically, floods have been seen as a major obstacle to economic development. Attempts to control rivers have a long and somewhat chequered history. If the destruction of wetlands and forests can unintentionally increase river flooding, what about building in rivers and on floodplains? In the USA, as in many other countries, floodplains have been a focus of development. People need to live near rivers for water, agriculture, transportation and waste disposal.

A wide range of navigation and flood-control structures has been built on many major American rivers, including:

- **dams**, which create lakes for irrigation, navigation and flood control

- **levées** (dykes built parallel to the flow), which constrain the river, help to form deep navigation channels and offer some protection to land in the floodplain
- **wing dykes** built at right-angles to the direction of flow, which increase velocity and promote bed scour, making navigation easier

There is an extensive system of locks, dams and levées on the Mississippi and Missouri Rivers, which drain most of the USA.

To farmers, transport companies and property owners, levées are critical for taming the rivers; to environmentalists, they are artificial restraints that encourage development and farming in the floodplain. The natural role of a floodplain is to carry excess water during periods of heavy runoff. However, when the floodplain is walled off behind levées, the artificially narrowed river must rise higher to compensate for lack of ability to spread out laterally. And while levées do protect farms and towns during minor floods, the flood of 1993 demonstrated that giant floods can still reclaim the floodplain, no matter how high the levées.

Opponents of river management say that the logical move is to leave the floodplain and move away from rivers that cannot be controlled. After the 1993 flood, several towns were relocated above the Mississippi and Missouri River floodplains. However, development is continuing in the floodplain — malls and homes are being built behind restored levées. When a large flood event comes along, these restored levées are likely to break.

Hydro-electric power

Hydro-electric schemes have long been central features of regional development projects. The Tennessee Valley Authority of 1933 was the 'father' of all subsequent schemes, many of which have been central to economic development policies. The reasoning runs as follows:

- Creating a more dependable water resource for agriculture improves yields. This increases farm income, permitting greater investment and mechanisation, which releases labour from the land.
- The dam produces cheap electricity, attracting industries that use the labour released from the land. Industries which require a lot of power, such as aluminium production and chemicals, attract other industries that use these materials.
- Regional take-off is achieved, accelerated by the multiplier effect.

Hydro-electric power plants convert the kinetic energy contained in falling water into electricity. The energy in flowing water is ultimately derived from the sun and is therefore constantly being renewed. Energy in sunlight evaporates water from the oceans and deposits it on land in the form of rain. Differences in land elevation result in rainfall runoff and allow some of the original solar energy to be captured as hydro-electric power.

Hydro-electric power is currently the world's largest renewable source of electricity, accounting for 6% of the worldwide energy supply — about 15% of the world's electricity. For example, in Canada, hydro-electric power is abundant, supplying 60% of all electrical needs. It was traditionally thought of as a cheap and clean source of electricity, but many large hydro-electric schemes being planned today are meeting opposition from environmental groups and native peoples.

There is much unused hydro-electric power potential in LEDCs. For example, in China, only 12% of the estimated hydro-electric power potential has been developed. It supplies about 19% of power needs, while 80% is supplied by coal. The plan is to increase hydro-electric power to 40% of the supply by 2020. Most potential lies in the upper Yangtze and western rivers, including the controversial Three Gorges Dam Project.

Although hydro-electric schemes appear to be less troublesome in terms of pollution and sustainability than burning fossil fuels, they displace large numbers of people who are often poor and politically weak. However, powerful campaigns against such schemes have been organised in countries as politically diverse as China, Brazil and India.

River management issues

The Mekong

The Mekong River is the longest in southeast Asia. From its source in China near the border with Tibet, the Mekong flows generally southeast to the South China Sea, a distance of 4200 km. It crosses Yunnan Province, China, forming the border between Myanmar (Burma) and Laos and most of the border between Laos and Thailand. It then flows through Cambodia and southern Vietnam into a rich delta, before emptying into the South China Sea. There are steep descents and swift rapids in the upper course, but the river is navigable south of Louangphrabang in Laos. The Mekong flows through several countries, so the issues of river management are especially significant — decisions made in one country will impact in others.

The management issues and priorities vary from country to country, as do the level of development and the populations. In northeast Thailand, with over 20 million people, the water resources are well developed. Partly as a consequence of this, problems are emerging associated with salinisation of arable lands as a result of clearing natural vegetation and poor irrigation. Laos (5 million people) is a much poorer country and the water resources are as yet undeveloped. Cambodia (10 million people) is recovering from 40 years of war. In the Mekong delta, some 20 million Vietnamese live on some of the most highly productive agricultural land in the world.

The Colorado

The Colorado River drains nearly one-twelfth of the US continent. In the past it was developed to promote irrigated agriculture and the river now provides water for a range of uses, including domestic and agricultural, for diverse groups and individuals. As the principal river in an arid region, it has always been vital to life. However, while its consumptive values for agriculture and drinking water remain high, over recent decades the river's water has come to mean more than economic prosperity.

Increasingly, the Colorado provides recreation and adds aesthetic value in a rapidly urbanising region. For more than 800 km, the river flows through national park lands. Drinking water demands from rapidly growing regional populations and Native

American water rights claims increase demands on the river. Threatened or endangered native species occur in many sections of the river. The rising importance of non-consumptive uses and the recognition of the need to protect cultural and natural resources complicate management.

Fifty years ago, the challenge was harnessing the river to deliver its water efficiently. Today, the challenges are greater, and river management is undergoing change. There are complicated and sometimes controversial issues about who should have the greatest claim to the water, while there have been fundamental changes in the economics and demographics of the region. The basin itself remains largely rural and agricultural, though fast-growing urban areas dominate the surrounding regions — a city such as Las Vegas has high water consumption, often for extravagances such as watering golf courses in the desert.

> **Exam tip** The demands described above made by a rapidly growing urban population on a water resource in an arid climate might be usefully compared with those of Egypt and the Nile. It is a useful reminder that the consequences of rapid urban growth are not confined to LEDCs and that the arguments over scarce resources may be almost as fierce between states within a nation state as they are between nation states themselves.

Coastal processes can be managed

Over the last 50 years, the need for coastal management has increased.

- The coastal zone has the most complex and fragile environmental, resource and physical systems on Earth.
- A nation's coastal zone is frequently its most valued and contentious area.
- Almost half the world's population lives within 150 km of a coastline.
- Important tropical coastal resources and environments continue their downward spirals of degradation, non-sustainable levels of exploitation, elimination and extinction.
- The growing reality of global sea-level rise poses both short-term and long-term problems for almost all coastal regions.

Sea level is rising at an increasing rate worldwide. It is estimated that along the Gulf and Atlantic coasts of the USA, a 30 cm rise in sea level is likely by 2050. In the next century, a 1–2 m rise is possible. Sea level will probably continue to rise for several centuries, even if global temperatures stop rising a few decades hence.

Rising sea level inundates wetlands and other low-lying lands, erodes beaches, intensifies flooding, and increases the salinity of rivers, bays and groundwater tables. Other aspects of climate change may further exacerbate some of these effects. Measures that people take to protect private property from rising sea level may have adverse effects on the environment and on public use of beaches and waterways.

State and local governments are already starting to take measures to prepare for the consequences of rising sea level.

The need for coastal management

The Atlantic coast of New England

Almost all the coastal communities of New England have restated their intent to hold the line on their residential land and on all developed areas; very few advocate drawing back in a managed retreat.

Various sectors of the coastal zone — tourism, fishing, the salt marshes (which nurture young fish), water supply and the threat of rising insurance rates — are important to the region's economy. They have suffered a 40 cm sea-level rise over the past century; there might be as much as a 2 m rise in the next century. Since 1980, ten northeasterly storms and several hurricanes have hit the heavily populated coastline. The coast is constantly changing. Flooding is increasing both in area and amount of damage caused.

From 1870 to 1920, the weather was comparatively calm; there were no storms and summer residences were built up and down the coast. In 1920, there was a ferocious northeasterly storm. In 1944, a severe hurricane destroyed all the timber jetties and yet another large storm struck in March 1962. All of this pales into insignificance compared with the storms of the past 20 years. Storms that once would have been rated as 100-year storms now appear every 30 years.

In common with many coastal regions of MEDCs, one response to rising sea level, and the increasing cost of protecting the shoreline, has been to advocate managed retreat so that 'good money is not thrown after bad' by trying to prevent the inevitable. However, after years of watching their beaches crumble and wash away and following many expensive, and often pointless, efforts to halt the damage, the coastal communities of this coastline still do not agree on solutions. There has been polarisation in the past between:

- those who favour public expenditure to hold back the sea
- those who are sceptical about erosion-fighting programmes
- those who believe people should not be allowed to rebuild in hazardous areas

Exam tip This issue is complex because the prediction of future change is central to making decisions about current policy. Predictions are notoriously unreliable and it is easy to find sceptics who do not believe in human-generated global warming and who have a different view about coastal management.

Bangladesh

Bangladesh has more than 24 000 km of rivers and canals that cover more than 7% of the country's land area. Most parts of the country are linked by a network of waterways that expands in the monsoon period. Only a fraction of these waterways is navigable.

Three major rivers (the Ganges, Brahmaputra and Meghna) join the sea in Bangladesh and they dominate the country. Together, these rivers form the world's largest delta. High sediment load and highly variable discharge cause serious problems for navigation and for the management, operation and development of the whole river system.

Sudden and largely unpredictable changes in water depth due to deposition during falling discharge periods, and the rapid migration of channels during flood periods, are common events. These are largely caused by natural processes, but are made worse by human interference, much of which takes place in other countries through which the rivers flow, such as India and Nepal. This raises issues of international law and equity between countries. The use of water for irrigation, deforestation in the river basin and discharge of chemical waste into the river are all occurring beyond the national boundaries of Bangladesh as well as within the country, causing deteriorating water quality and highly 'flashy' discharge. Within the country, water is also being abstracted from groundwater by tube-wells and from rivers by low-lift pumps, resulting in reduced stream flow and even more sedimentation.

Bangladesh has one of the most densely populated, low-lying coastal zones in the world, with 20–25 million people living within a 1 m elevation of the high-tide level. In general, the topography of the country is flat, except for marginal hills in the north-east and southeast regions. The *average* land elevation is about 7.5 m above mean sea level. As a consequence, most waterways are under tidal influence. The coastline in Bangladesh totals about 735 km, of which 125 km are covered by the Sunderbans — a major natural mangrove forest.

The sectors of Bangladesh's coastal activities identified as most vulnerable to climate change and sea level change are agriculture, aquaculture, fisheries, forestry and tourism. The possible effects of sea-level change are inundation, salt-water intrusion, flash floods, droughts and storm surges.

Management issues

The management of marine, coastal and estuarine environments is an important component of government in all countries with a coastline, especially in MEDCs that have the resources to invest in such strategies. Opportunities for these environments are explored in terms of management strategies to promote the principles of ecologically sustainable development and the protection and development of specific coastal resources. Management issues include:

- beach replenishment
- protection of sensitive areas
- tourism development
- coastal and marina development
- coastal residential development
- revegetation and weed eradication programmes
- education
- local government involvement and community programmes
- climate change and sea-level rise, and their effects on coastal processes
- water quality
- pollution and waste management
- wildlife management

Resource management and conservation means minimising the impact of port and residential development, oil transportation and runoff pollution. To deal with coastal problems, many management policies attempt to oversee almost all activities on the coast, from adding a new porch to a private home to building a new refinery.

Synoptic links from Unit 2

Governments have a direct and indirect influence on population change

Censuses

Information about a country's population growth, characteristics, living conditions, distribution and physical resources is essential for the development of policy, planning and implementation. The collection and analysis of population and development data is a fundamental part of government activity in every state. Over the past two decades, many LEDCs have made real progress in obtaining such data, matching those gathered for almost a century in MEDCs.

Planners need population and development data to:

- assess demographic trends
- assess the socioeconomic situation of women
- design population policies, strategies and programmes
- integrate population factors into development planning
- monitor and evaluate the effectiveness of policies and programmes in the light of national and international development goals
- help promote population awareness among government decision makers and the population at large

These tasks require a vast body of information, which, in turn, requires a national statistical institutional framework, as well as training and research in demographic and statistical methods.

The data collected are not perfect. Under-enumeration (under-counting) is a well-known phenomenon in even the most advanced societies, particularly in urban areas where people are frequently on the move and not always keen to be 'counted'. In the UK, for example, no census form was returned from about 3.0% of the population in 1991. Some households were missed by enumerators and some people were not included in census returns, particularly those who slept 'rough'. The Census Coverage Survey has estimated that this represents a further 1.8% of the population. Thus it is estimated that about 95% of the population responded to the 2001 census.

The UK census

The 2001 census of the UK counted almost 60 million people in approximately 24 million households. It asked 40 questions and produced over 2 billion items of information to guide public spending of £50 billion each year.

Two centuries of census taking have produced a record of remarkable change in British society. For example, in 1931, 16% of the population lived in urban areas compared with 90% in 2001. The average size of households has halved in 100 years, from 4.6 persons in 1901 to 2.4 persons today. We are living longer — in 1821, almost half the population was under 20 years of age compared with just over 25% today.

When it started many people objected to census taking on religious grounds — it was an unhappy reminder to Christians of the Roman census of the Holy Land. Others feared that the data collected would give away too much information to enemies. Some saw it as an intrusion on civil liberties as the state grew in power, which has echoes in the objections to identity cards today. The first UK census was approved by Parliament in an atmosphere of fear, after the publication of Malthus's essay on population and the dreadful harvest of 1800, which many thought to be a precursor of famine.

Over the past 200 years, census questions have developed to reflect changes in society. In the 2001 census, a question about religion was added, which reflects the fact that increasing numbers of people identify themselves in terms of their religion. Historical examples of new questions include the addition of a question about the number of rooms in each household in 1891, in response to worries about overcrowding in industrial cities. A question about 'journey to work' was introduced in 1921, as people moved out of cities to the suburbs and began to take more bus and train journeys.

Census information has been important in planning public policy. For example, in 1851 detailed data available from the census were used to classify people by occupation and age. A government statistician concluded that 'miners die in undue proportions...tailors die in considerable numbers at younger ages'. Such results had an impact on politicians and added fuel to the movements for social reform. The census was thus a largely progressive phenomenon.

Other censuses
Britain was by no means the first country to take a census. The ancient Babylonians, Chinese, Egyptians and Romans all collected statistics about their people for taxation purposes. In more modern times, Quebec completed a census as early as 1666; Iceland in 1703.

The reliability of census information varies greatly. In some countries, self-completion is not possible because of illiteracy. It is not possible to say how inaccurate the data are, but ± 5% is a fair margin to allow. Gaps in data hamper efforts to formulate evidence-based policies, design programmes and channel resources to those most in need. Accurate population information and statistics are indispensable in studying how demographic trends are affected by, and have an impact on, social, economic and environmental factors. Major gaps exist in the following areas:

- population issues
- women's reproductive health
- women's work
- migration — particularly at regional and international levels
- the effects of population growth and distribution on poverty, the environment and natural resources

Population policies

Governments can adopt one of three attitudes or sets of policies with respect to their population:

- pronatal view — an increase in fertility is promoted

- antinatal view — a decrease in fertility is promoted
- neutral view — population growth is not an issue

Governments can attempt to change population trends using:

- exhortation — women (and men) are encouraged or discouraged from having children
- fiscal policies (especially tax rates) — either promoting or discouraging large families
- social policies — the provision of day care or generous maternity leave
- coercive policies — punishing women (and men) for having too many children
- migration policies — encouraging or discouraging population loss or gain

Pronatal policies

The motives for increasing the birth rate are complex, but include:

- compensation for war-time losses, for example France after 1918
- the preservation of a labour force in the light of an ageing population, for example modern Japan
- the promotion of a particular race in pursuit of racially motivated policies, for example Nazi Germany in the 1930s
- frontier development, for example modern Brazil, with its large areas of under-exploited resources

Antinatal policies

Voluntary policies to curb birth rates occurred in India and Pakistan in the 1950s. They included spreading of education and information about family planning clinics. Indonesia had 2000 clinics, funded by the government with aid from the World Health Organization (WHO), World Bank and United Nations (UN) and promoted through the mass media and fieldworkers. Since 1976, there has been a rapid drop in total fertility rate. Land reform and the improvement in the legal status of women have had similar effects in Kerala (southern India), where a Marxist dominated regional government saw poverty as a key factor in the high birth rate and attempted to implement reforms to eradicate extremes of wealth.

At the height of population increase, many countries have resorted to **coercive policies**. One of the best-known examples in a democracy is from India, which introduced a compulsory sterilisation programme in 1976. This brought down the government in the following year. Even better known is the one-child policy pursued in China. Following rapid population growth in the 1950s and 1960s, by the 1970s China was experiencing a severe population problem, hindering its rapid progress towards industrialisation and development. The communist regime imposed a two-child policy, revised to a one-child policy in 1980, with certain exceptions. Policies to promote this included:

- postponing the age of marriage to 26 for women and 28 for men
- free contraceptives and abortions
- strong peer pressure
- higher levels of education for women
- a social safety net

There were severe financial and social penalties for non-compliance, including loss of promotion opportunity, loss of food subsidies, reduction in housing quality and fines. Forced sterilisation was also carried out. As a result, China's population growth and fertility rate fell dramatically.

Year	Population increase	Fertility rate
1971	2.4 %	5.4
1985	1.1 %	1.6

Today, only 17% of Chinese families have just one child.

Exam tip It is much easier for a non-democratic state, such as China, to impose a policy of coercive population control than it is for a democratic state, such as India.

The case of Singapore

Population planning in Singapore is related to economic planning. The island is only 536 km^2 in area and has very few natural resources; therefore, the physical carrying capacity is very small. To overcome this limitation, the government adopted economic and population planning policies. The 'stop-at-two' population policy of 1965–87 was designed to support economic plans to improve the quality of life of the people. Restraint in population growth was sold to the public as a necessary move, serving the good of the country, as it struggled to build a nation in the early years of independence.

However, in 1983, Singapore changed from being antinatal to being pronatal. Increasingly, it concentrated its economy on high value-added service products, such as merchant banking and currency markets, using the new information age of computers to take advantage of globalisation. In order to exploit this potential advantage it needed skilled labour — hence the new 'have-three-or-more-if-you-can-afford-it' policy.

Exam tip Singapore is a very good example of how changing values and attitudes can lead to a reversal of policy — in this case from an almost Malthusian view to that argued by Ester Boserup. Alternatively, one could read it as support for the view that different periods need different policies.

Government policies influence settlement characteristics and patterns

The terms rural and urban are difficult to define. They can be differentiated on the basis of:

- the size of the settlements
- the function of the settlements

Definition by size has never been easy. Agricultural settlements on the Hungarian plain or in West Africa may have more than 10 000 inhabitants, whereas some English market towns with distinctive central place functions might have populations of only 5000. In recent years, with the decline of agricultural employment in many countries, the distinction has become more difficult. Several trends are notable:

- **Counterurbanisation** is the process by which the urban population moves out into rural areas, either following employment or to commute into the city.
- Counterurbanisation is closely related to **urban sprawl**, which has produced distinctive and essentially new urban landscapes in the USA.
- The increasing levels of mechanisation in agriculture and the subsequent decline of a distinctively rural employment structure have been matched by a decline in other rural employment, such as forestry and fishing.
- The increase in leisure and tourist activities in most MEDCs has changed the nature of the 'countryside' as a resource.

The role of government in managing the environment has grown remarkably. Even in nation states such as the USA, where the increasing role of government is constantly under attack, both central and local government hold a considerable range of powers.

Managing urban sprawl in the USA

Most North American cities were built using technologies that assumed an inexhaustible supply of cheap oil and land. These communities grew with low-density distribution of populations compared with most European cities of medieval origin and they became increasingly dependent on transport. Cheap energy encouraged an infatuation with the automobile and increased the separation of work places from homes.

Urban sprawl is the legacy of abundant oil and an assumed right to unrestricted use of the private car, whatever the social costs and externalities. Per capita, petrol consumption in many cities in the USA and Canada is now more than four times that of European cities. It is over 10 times greater than that in high-density cities such as Hong Kong and Tokyo. These differences in consumption are partially explained by larger car sizes and lower petrol prices. However, differences in the compactness of land-use patterns are more important. Sprawling suburbs are arguably the most economically, environmentally and socially costly pattern of residential development humans have ever devised.

The negative local and regional consequences of sprawl (e.g. congestion, urban air pollution and commuting distances) are now widely recognised. Many of these external costs fall unevenly on the population. Less widely acknowledged are the global ramifications of North American land-use patterns. Largely because of low-density sprawl, the residents of American cities produce about twice as much carbon dioxide per capita as do Amsterdam residents.

The argument about sprawl is one of the fiercest in the USA, with many defenders of the civil liberty to live in whatever environment one chooses. There is no consensus. The development, building and real estate industries are powerful voices that defend sprawl against hostile environmentalist critics.

A study in San José, California, compared the environmental demands of 13 000 new residential units contained within an urban 'greenbelt' with the same number if they had been built in the usual sprawl pattern. The sprawl homes would require 320 000 more km of car commuting and 11 million more litres of water per day. The sprawl units would also require 40% more energy for heating and cooling than would their urban counterparts.

Exam tip Sprawl is not confined to the United States. The current growth of Manila or Jakarta is dominated by low-density outward spread, which is creating major problems of urban congestion. In MEDCs, road planners tend to react to such growth by improving the roads to solve the congestion, which, in turn, generates more sprawl. This is a good example of positive feedback.

The problems of urban sprawl can be contained by:

- setting planning limits on physical expansion
- favouring and promoting alternatives to the private car
- limiting car access in inner cities
- applying regional carbon dioxide taxes
- restricting parking availability
- using traffic-calming street designs

Britain's New Towns: an experiment in urban planning

In 1946, the New Towns programme was launched to create a series of new communities across Britain. These were a planned reaction to concerns about urban sprawl and the risks to the countryside around the major conurbations. They were also part of a wider plan to relocate enterprise and industry away from inner-city areas. Many of them were designated to encircle London's green belt.

Each New Town was to work both independently and in cooperation with other towns. It was seen as an opportunity to put Britain's architectural and environmental knowledge into a 'perfect' setting, to create an urban Utopia.

It is now more than 50 years since the New Town Act paved the way for what Lord Reith described at the time as 'an essay in civilisation'. People who moved to the New Towns in the early stages of their development have seen the towns grow.

Whether or not the New Towns of the 1940s and 1950s were a success is open to subjective interpretation. However, even their most loyal defenders wince a little at what has become of towns such as Cumbernauld.

Not all the New Towns were built solely for the purpose of re-housing inner-city citizens. Although most were designed to cope with the overcrowding of the big cities, some of the towns were built for other reasons. For example:

- Newton Aycliffe was intended to act as an industrial magnet to attract business and commerce to County Durham.
- Corby in Northamptonshire was built to house an influx of workers for the nearby, rapidly expanding, steelworks. The steelworks have now closed.

The most recent spate of New Towns, begun in the early 1960s, includes Skelmersdale near Liverpool, Telford near Shrewsbury and Milton Keynes, approximately 50 km northwest of Greater London.

By 1985, most of the New Town development corporations' work was complete. All the town centres had long been established, as had the older neighbourhoods. The creation of the New Towns had seen many new ideas and unique architectural designs, including:

- pedestrianised town centres, such as those in Crawley and Stevenage
- development of single-function neighbourhoods
- networks of cycle tracks
- specific public transport routes

Exam tip New Towns were built in the period when the separation of functions into discrete neighbourhoods was almost a mantra of urban planning. Therefore, residential areas were poorly served with services and town centres were dominated by retail and office functions. By the late 1980s, this idea had become discredited because town centres were abandoned in the evenings and residential areas lacked vitality for much of the day. Changing attitudes and values have had a profound influence on the way towns and cities look.

There were designs put forward that were not carried out. For example, in Crawley New Town, a plan was put forward to build a garage or parking plot for every home. The idea was rejected on the grounds that the low probability of usage did not warrant the high costs involved; an argument that now seems somewhat shortsighted. At the time, the report explained that the likelihood of the increase in car ownership sustaining itself at the then current rate was improbable and to spend such a large amount of money on an entirely car-oriented society would be unwise.

Exam tip There are few better examples of how planners can get it so dreadfully wrong! However, at the time the decision was made, very few people would have expected that the disposable income of an average family would rise as fast as it has. Planning infrastructure is littered with similar examples, from the first Severn Bridge to the M25, both of which reached their capacity in a far shorter time period than that predicted. In the case of the M25, plans were being made to add more lanes within weeks of it opening.

Planning and gender issues in LEDCs

Urban planning

Many women in LEDCs have to work in or near the home, so they are the people most affected by failures in the planning of housing and settlement projects. Examples of bad urban planning that fail to consider women's needs are:

- the absence of day-care facilities
- the inappropriate location of public water points in poor communities
- the lack of children's play parks
- inadequate lighting of streets and public areas
- costly and inconvenient public transport facilities
- 'modern' housing designs that do not take into consideration women's traditional use of space
- zoning laws that prohibit economic activities and food-growing in residential areas, disrupting women's income-producing strategies

LEDCs that have made major advances in insuring housing for women include India and Namibia:

- In India, women have gained legal rights to inherit land and property. However, gender inequalities still persist as women's shares are often smaller than those of men. In a major breakthrough, the government of Maharashtra state recognised the right of slum and pavement dwellers to shelter. Through collective ownership, communities will be able to obtain security of tenure. Women's participation is an integral element of the programme.
- Namibia is expecting repeal of laws that require married women to obtain their husbands' signature, but the practice of human settlement policy has already changed. The government is active in designing and implementing housing programmes that are gender-sensitive. They encourage women to form saving and credit groups.

In many parts of Africa, deeply entrenched patriarchal traditions and values dictate that wealth, property and land belong to men. In such social systems, women do not inherit or own land or property because customarily these belong to husbands or fathers and it is the sons who inherit. A woman is perceived as a 'temporary resident' in her parents' home until she gets married and as a resident in her husband's home, so long as he is alive and satisfied with her. This means that when a man dies, his widow suffers a double tragedy — she not only loses her partner but also the material wealth the couple owned. The property and land are claimed by her in-laws, leaving her with none of the wealth she helped to create.

If the widow is childless or has no sons, she may be evicted from the land and forced to return to her parents. If the widow has children, particularly sons, she could continue to stay on the land because her sons will inherit it.

Exam tip Ironically, in most African countries the law does not discriminate against women in land or property ownership. Indeed, national laws in many countries give women equal rights to men. However, the reality is different because of traditions, customs and attitudes that have existed for centuries. This is a useful qualifying example to use when discussing government policies.

Managing urban decay in the UK

The declining significance of manufacturing in most MEDCs, and the increasing mechanisation of the manufacturing base, posed problems for many of Britain's inner-city areas, which suffered loss of both employment opportunities and population from the 1950s onwards. In turn, this led to a cycle of multiple deprivation in which the negative multiplier effect led to further loss of employment, income and social services. Policy reaction to this decline evolved as follows:

- There were attempts to improve the social wellbeing of the population. The Plowden Report, published in 1967, identified uneven educational achievement as a major problem. This was followed by Community Development projects and the establishment of Development Agencies. This marked a change in policy because, until this time, New Towns had been the focus of attention. Economic decline in inner-city areas was recognised officially by the government in 1977.

- Riots in Brixton, Toxteth and other inner-city areas stimulated the establishment of Urban Development Corporations, initially for London and Merseyside, followed in the late 1980s by eight other UDCs.
- In the 1990s, a new set of policies emerged that stressed public–private partnerships and moved away from large-scale regional grants towards improvement of the skill level of the population and to a more flexible planning system that gives priority to business over other competing land-uses, such as residence. The Social Enterprise Unit was set up in 2001 and tax credits for disadvantaged neighbourhoods began in 2003.

However, after almost half a century of attention by government at all levels the inner cities remain some of the poorest areas in Britain. The new initiatives have not been a total success; neither has the new policy of community-centred action. For example, in Shoreditch, northeast London, the community wanted to repair council houses, but keep them in council ownership. However, the government rejected the plan as unsustainable and the community was asked to consider transferring the homes to a housing association. Local community wishes were confounded by central government.

Exam tip There are many issues here, not the least of which is the ethnic division in British society. Many of the most deprived inner-city areas are dominated by either Asian or Afro-Caribbean communities who have frequently expressed, through their community leaders, a sense of neglect and distance from the decision-making processes.

In the view of almost all observers, Britain needs more houses and the current battleground is between the regeneration of brownfield sites (many in inner cities) and the use of greenfield sites, which is often preferred by developers. The private sector is only producing a small fraction of the housing the nation needs, as social change, rather than population increase, fuels the demand. Fiscal measures and the planning system should be used to exploit sites that already have planning permission but which for various reasons are undeveloped.

Exam tip The private sector has never been very good at providing cheap housing because the profit margins are larger on four 'executive' homes (e.g. £400 000 each) than they are on 10 'starter' homes (e.g. £160 000 each) on the same area of land. Therefore, the state has always had to devise systems whereby housing demand can be met. If this does not happen, trailer parks will grow to serve the need, as in the USA.

The Thames Gateway has 12 000 hectares of undeveloped land. Government has to be involved in projects of this magnitude, in which large-scale issues of decontamination, drainage, public transport and so on must be dealt with efficiently and where whole communities can be created.

Government policies influence migration patterns

Very few issues arouse such strong emotions as immigration. Governments are obliged to take a view and to be seen to be active in pursuing a well-defined policy or risk losing significant support. The argument about immigration policy is complex, clouded by misconceptions, and readily fuelled by racial myths.

In almost all MEDCs, there are people who argue that immigration should be more restricted. Among the diverse reasons advanced for greater restriction are the views that:

- A country should remain predominantly of one race. Continued immigration threatens the numerical and cultural predominance of that race, which is usually white.
- The present immigrant stream (at least at the low-wage end) is a 'low-quality' stream. Many immigrants arriving in MEDCs have few skills or assets to contribute.
- The present immigrant stream (or certain parts of it) is a 'high-defect' stream. Many immigrants arriving in MEDCs bring problems with them, including diseases and habits of poverty, drugs, illiteracy and a tendency towards crime.
- Continued immigration will exert a downward pressure on the wages and working conditions of workers already in the country. This applies particularly to those towards the bottom of the economic ladder, who are most likely to be in direct competition with low-skill immigrants.
- A country such as Britain welcoming high-skill immigrants encourages a brain-drain from poorer countries. Such countries need to keep their native talent for national development.
- There is simply not enough to go around. The receiving country cannot afford to share its wealth with the people who want to come in from poorer neighbours.

Exam tip The above arguments are sometimes mutually contradictory and will not all be held by any single person or interest group.

On the other hand, some people argue that immigration should be more generously permitted than it is at present. Among the diverse reasons advanced for greater liberalisation are the views that:

- Past immigration restrictions operated with a strong racial bias. It would be good for a country (economically, socially and culturally) to have a wide ethnic mix.
- The present immigrant stream (including the low-wage end) is a 'high-quality' stream. Many immigrants arriving in MEDCs have characteristics that make them particularly valuable to the receiving economy. Various commentators see different characteristics as desirable. Examples of desirable characteristics include:
  - strong work ethic
  - an admirable devotion to family
  - deep religious convictions
  - entrepreneurship
  - powerful traditions of labour organisation and community improvement
  - a willingness to perform work despised by indigenous workers
  - enthusiasm for a job — working without complaint
- Increased immigration flow will help discipline indigenous workers and encourage them to give up their short-sighted insistence on high wages and soft working conditions. Therefore, they will be more eager to pitch in, making their employers more efficient and productive competitors in the global economy.

- Increased immigration flow will help indigenous workers learn about, and empathise with, their fellow workers around the world. Workers share many important interests and experiences, despite divisions of race, culture, language and income.
- Present low-wage immigrant workers are likely to be politically active fighters against injustice. They will bring knowledge and energy to the task of winning greater democracy and economic justice for those towards the bottom of the economic heap.
- Freedom of movement is a basic human right. It should be recognised and protected in the global society, either in all instances or at least where capital and goods are flowing freely across borders.
- All MEDCs have a responsibility to accept (certain) immigrants and refugees. MEDCs may have played a powerful role in creating the conditions that have produced migration flow, sometimes as a result of military activity, sometimes as a result of economic policies that the MEDCs have urged, or forced, on the 'sending' countries.
- Attempts to keep immigrants out of the MEDCs are doomed to failure, given the social, economic, geographic and technological realities of today's global economy. Continued insistence on such restrictions will only lead to further removal of fundamental rights for all citizens.

Exam tip It is very hard to find much middle ground here. The possibility of consensus is remote. Migration arouses powerful emotions and governments have to be responsive to that. In democracies, it is likely that newspaper campaigns and anecdotal information will carry at least as much weight as official statistics or logic. If one believes a country to be 'overpopulated', then attitudes to immigration are likely to be negative. However, if one believes that a country is short of skills and would profit from cultural diversity, then one is likely to be positively inclined to higher levels of immigration.

US immigration

Historical background

The USA was built upon in-migration yet it has a long history of regulating immigration. Early legislation tried to limit entry, but was strongly biased in favour of northern Europeans.

The Immigration and Nationality Act Amendments of 1965 established important principles that are still significant. The amendments led to changes in immigration policy. The national origins quota system as the basis for immigration was abolished and was replaced by a preference system for visas. Numbers were increased from 154 000 to 290 000, of which 120 000 were reserved for immigrants from the western hemisphere.

In this period, the USA started to experience a more varied entry geography, with significant contributions from Asia and, particularly, Latin America.

In later developments, increasingly severe treatment of illegal immigration was put in place. Thus, in an attempt to 'close the back door while opening the front door', the government granted amnesty to illegal immigrants who had lived in the USA for a significant period of time and tried to slow down illegal immigration by making it harder to employ illegal immigrants and more costly if one was caught doing so. Border controls were also stepped up, especially with Mexico.

Impact of the new migrants

Over the past 50 years the number of foreign-born people in the US has increased dramatically. In 2000, 28.4 million (excluding illegal immigrants) lived in the US, representing approximately 10% of the population. In terms of absolute numbers, this was a record high. The estimated number of illegal immigrants was 5 million. Hence, the total number was over 33 million, or about 11% of the population (still lower than the 15% highs that occurred in both 1890 and 1910).

According to US Census Bureau 2000 Current Population Survey data, 51% of these foreign-born persons originated from Latin America (including Central America, South America and the Caribbean), 25.7% from Asia, 15.2% from Europe and 8.1% from other regions of the world, such as Africa and Oceania. Migrants from Central America (including, for data purposes, Mexico) accounted for nearly one-third of the entire foreign-born population. Mexicans, the largest single group, now comprise 27% of all foreign-born persons in the USA. They also constitute the largest proportion of the illegal immigrant population by far, distantly followed by people from El Salvador and then Guatemala. At 12.5%, Hispanics now form the largest ethnic minority group in the US.

> **Exam tip** The attitude to illegal immigrants in the USA is ambivalent. On the one hand, there are serious concerns about the impact of a large number of untraceable and undocumented immigrants (especially since 9/11) but, on the other hand, they provide one of the cheapest and least vocal sources of labour.

Refugees

In common with many other MEDCs, the USA has a refugee resettlement programme. There is an annual ceiling imposed by the government, and refugee admissions are distributed throughout the country.

The ceiling 'height' varies. For example, in 1999, admissions were increased from 78 000 to 91 000 to accommodate Kosovan refugees, while the ceiling for 2002 was 70 000. In addition, the 1994 agreement with Cuba allows 20 000 Cuban immigrants through legal channels.

The attacks of 11 September 2001 have altered public attitudes, and therefore affected government perception of immigration policy. In broad terms, the 'war on terrorism' has encouraged opponents of immigration to step up their campaign to restrict entry into the USA.

> **Exam tip** Increasingly broad measures to prevent or intercept terrorist activities passed after the 9/11 attacks have been a source of concern for some immigrant and civil liberties groups. In the coming decade, exploration of the relationship between the threat of terror, public fears and challenge of civil liberties by more restrictive legislation will be closely examined.

The economic prospects of the USA and other MEDCs with more or less full employment and a shortage of skills will remain strongly tied to immigration forces. In the USA, immigrants comprise 13.5% of the population aged 16 and over and account for nearly the same percentage of the labour force. During the latter half of the 1990s, immigrants of all legal statuses contributed a net 35% to the total growth in numbers, while the number of foreign-born workers increased by nearly 25% compared with just 5% for all native-born workers.

The refugee experience in Canada

Like the USA, Canada is a country built around immigration. It is the product of several hundred years of in-migration that transformed a region previously occupied only sparsely by Native Americans. The controversy that has surrounded the admission of refugees to Canada in recent years is not unique to Canada — it mirrors a much larger debate taking place in other parts of the world. For example, across western Europe, in the USA and in parts of Asia, many governments have introduced restrictive measures to control the flow of refugees into their countries. This legislative activity has been both the cause of, and a response to, a growing awareness of the problems and challenges posed by refugees. It is a recognition that these difficulties are not only mounting, but that they are also substantially different from those that existed in 1951, when the international community adopted the Convention Relating to the Status of Refugees. Many elements characterise this new situation, but two principal features can be readily identified:

- The world's population of refugees has grown at an unprecedented rate in recent years, increasing over the last decade to between 11 million and 15 million — a total that strains the capacity of the international community to adapt.
- The increasing ease of transport has made many more countries accessible to refugee flows — to their alarm, many have been turned into countries of first refuge.

Migration and resettlement inevitably result in loss of the sense of home and belonging that is critical to achieving an optimal level of health and wellbeing. Although people who choose to migrate to Canada do experience this loss (along with the many challenges associated with resettlement), their experience is not usually as difficult as that of refugees who are forced to leave their countries of origin and have no choice over their destination.

Refugees come to Canada to escape:

- natural disaster or war
- persecution because of their race, religion, gender, nationality, political viewpoint, sexual orientation or membership of a particular social group

Their experiences often lead to severe emotional trauma that scars them for life.

Refugees not only have different experiences, but are treated differently when they arrive. Convention refugees, or 'government-sponsored' refugees, have the prior approval of the Canadian government. As a result, they receive a number of federal benefits. Some refugees are privately sponsored by churches or other groups and receive the support they need through these private sponsors. About 50% of refugees are refugee claimants who apply for Convention status on arrival. Refugee claimants do not receive the federal benefits that Convention refugees do. When they have submitted their claims, refugee claimants are eligible for legal services, social assistance and some health services. However, many are not aware of these benefits. In addition, they are not allowed to sponsor family members (who may be stranded in refugee camps) until they become landed immigrants, which is often a long, drawn-out process.

Synoptic links from Unit 4

Weather and human activity are interdependent

The dominant view

The Earth's climate has always undergone change. Only 20 000 years ago, much of northern Europe was covered by a glacier that was up to 3 km thick. Sudden climate shifts occurred quite frequently during the Pleistocene, making the ice expand or contract. In the cold climate south of the ice-covered areas, small groups of people hunted reindeer, wild horses and bison. Over thousands of years, the Earth's orbit around the sun changed so that the summers became warmer and the ice began to melt. The last ice age ended around 10 000 years ago. Since then, the climate in the northern hemisphere has been warmer and more stable. Over the last 10 000 years of milder climate, people developed agriculture, then cities, and most recently industries. This has caused increasing emissions of carbon dioxide and other greenhouse gases. Many people expect that over the next 100 years we will see the fastest warming of the Earth since the end of the ice age.

The more we produce, consume and dispose of, the more we affect the environment. One global environmental problem is the risk of man-made climate change, particularly global warming.

Man-made climate change occurs because of the emission of greenhouse gases into the atmosphere. These emissions come from many sources, including agriculture and factories that supply us with food and other material goods, power stations that provide us with electricity, and cars and planes that take us where we want to go.

Greenhouse gases affect the Earth's climate by increasing the greenhouse effect. This is a natural phenomenon whereby water vapour, carbon dioxide and other gases in the atmosphere allow sunlight to pass through, but then absorb much of the heat reflected back from the Earth that otherwise would have escaped into space. Without the natural greenhouse effect, the mean temperature would be about −18°C and the Earth would be uninhabitable.

Emitting greenhouse gases increases the concentration of these gases in the atmosphere. This increases the greenhouse effect so that more heat is trapped by the atmosphere.

Evidence of changing climate

Global mean surface temperatures have increased by 0.5°C since the late nineteenth century (see Figure 2). The twentieth century's ten warmest years all occurred within the last 15 years of the century. Of these, 1998 was the warmest year on record. The snow cover in the northern hemisphere and floating ice in the Arctic Ocean have decreased. Globally, sea level has risen 100–120 mm over the past century. Worldwide precipitation over land has increased by about 1%. The frequency of extreme rainfall events has increased throughout much of the USA.

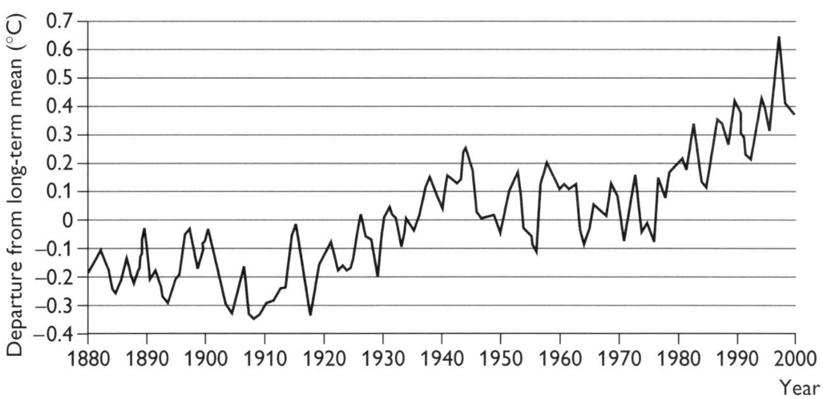

Figure 2 Global temperature changes (1880–2000)

Increasing concentrations of greenhouse gases are likely to accelerate the rate of climate change. Many scientists expect that the average global surface temperature could rise by 0.6–2.5°C in the next 50 years and 1.4–5.8°C in the next century, with significant regional variation. Evaporation will increase as the climate warms, which will increase average global precipitation. Soil moisture is likely to decline in many regions and intense rainstorms are likely to become more frequent. For example, sea level is likely to rise 60 cm along most of the US coast.

Exam tip One of the difficulties with the evidence is that it covers a limited number of years. Accurate records of global climate are only about 200 years old and there is much spatial variation that makes the reading of global trends difficult. The question that arises is, 'when does a sequential change become a trend?'

Links between ozone and global warming

Ozone gas is produced and found in a thin layer of the upper atmosphere. It absorbs harmful ultraviolet radiation from the sun. However, when polar stratospheric clouds form, reactions take place between ozone and chlorine, bromine and other halogen gases on the surface of ice or water droplets in these clouds, depleting the ozone. Most of those halogens are from chlorofluorocarbons emitted into the atmosphere by industrial processes. Thus a 'hole' has appeared in the ozone layer, at both poles. The loss of this protective layer has led to an increase in harmful radiation and is widely blamed for increases in the occurrence of skin cancers.

Though greenhouse gases cause atmospheric warming at the Earth's surface (the troposphere), they cool the higher-level stratosphere where the ozone occurs. Therefore, they are a likely cause of the increased ozone depletion because ozone chemistry is temperature-sensitive — very small changes in temperature have large effects on ozone production.

Exam tip Ozone is often confused with greenhouse gases. An understanding of the link between them will emphasise the distinction.

The sceptical view

Is global warming occurring?

- Given that climate is subject to many changes over time, the global air temperature increase of about 0.45°C over the past century may be no more than normal climatic variation. Bias in the data may in any case be responsible for some of this perceived increase.
- Some of the satellite data indicate a slight cooling in the climate over the last 18 years. These satellites use advanced technology and are not subject to the 'heat island' effect around major cities that affects ground-based thermometers.
- Projections of future climate change are uncertain. Although some computer models predict warming in the next century, these models are very limited. The effects of cloud formations, precipitation, the role of the oceans and the sun are still not well known and are often inadequately represented in the climatic models, although all play a major role in determining our climate. Scientists who work on these models are quick to point out that they are far from perfect representations of reality and are probably not advanced enough for direct use in policy implementation. Interestingly, as the computer-based climate models have become more sophisticated, the predicted increase in temperature has been reduced.

Are humans causing the climate to change?

- 98% of total global greenhouse gas emissions are natural (mostly water vapour); only 2% are from man-made sources.
- By most accounts, man-made emissions have had no more than a tiny impact on the climate. Although the climate has warmed slightly in the last 100 years, 70% of that warming occurred before 1940, i.e. before the upsurge in greenhouse gas emissions due to industrial processes.
- A recent survey indicated that only 17% of the members of the American Meteorological Society and the American Geophysical Society thought the warming of the nineteenth century was the result of an increase in greenhouse gas emissions.

If global warming occurs, will it be harmful?

- Larger quantities of carbon dioxide in the atmosphere and warmer climates would probably lead to an increase in vegetation. During warm periods in the past, vegetation flourished allowing, for instance, the Vikings to farm in now frozen Greenland and the English to have a flourishing wine industry — so perhaps the impacts would be positive rather than negative.

- The idea that global warming could melt the ice caps and flood coastal cities is highly controversial. An increase in global temperatures may not necessarily lead to a massive melting of the ice caps. Sea-level rises over the centuries have related more to warmer, expanding oceans than to melting ice caps.
- Some have argued that climatic warming will increase the spread of diseases. However, opponents argue that factors unrelated to climate change may have more impact on the spread of vector-borne diseases, such as:
  - deterioration in public health practices, such as rapid urbanisation without adequate infrastructure and forced large-scale resettlement of people
  - increased drug resistance
  - increased air travel
  - lack of insect-control programmes

Climatic events as hazards

Hazards have become both more frequent and more damaging in recent years. This is particularly true of climatic hazards. Part of the reason for the increase in damage is that there are more people living in the path of destructive hurricanes or tornadoes. Some people argue that the frequency of these events has increased and linkages have been made to global warming:

- Hurricanes are generated in areas where the seawater temperature is above 26°C.
- Global warming has increased the areas where this condition is met.
- Therefore, hurricanes have become more frequent.

The extreme climatic episodes of the late 1960s and early 1970s were assessed as a switch to a more variable and dangerous climate epoch, although the reason for this is uncertain. Irrespective of whether the global climate system has recently shifted to a more variable state, the *perception* that it has changed has stimulated studies of the impacts of extreme events and greater awareness of them.

Assessing the impact of natural hazards

In MEDCs, there has been a decrease in loss of life and an increase in economic losses as a result of natural hazards.

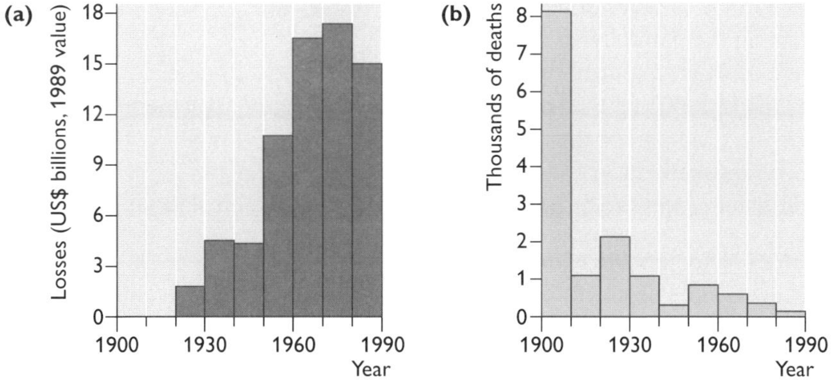

Figure 3 (a) Economic and (b) human losses to natural hazards in MEDCs

The capacity to survive and recover from the effects of a natural disaster is the result of:

- the physical magnitude of the disaster in a given area
- the social and economic conditions of individuals or social groups in that area — vulnerability varies between social groups in almost all natural disasters

Most natural catastrophes in 2002 were climate or weather related. They cost countries and communities an estimated $70 billion. Many of the disasters were related to the high level of rainfall; one-third of the 526 natural catastrophes were floods. In total, there were more windstorm-related natural disasters. However, floods killed more people and cost far more than windstorms, earthquakes or other natural catastrophes.

It is estimated that 90% of victims and 75% of all economic damage from natural hazards are in LEDCs, although it is worth remembering that the LEDCs also contain some 80% of the world population.

The relationship between socioeconomic conditions and the impact of natural disasters can be expressed in the following way:

- Economic constraints result in the poor being forced to live in precarious homes, made of flimsy, non-durable materials.
- These homes are located on the least-valued plots of land on steep hillsides, in floodplains, in fragile ecosystems and watersheds, on contaminated land, across rights-of-way and in other inappropriate areas.
- During disasters, poor management of services and inadequate infrastructure further complicate survival efforts.
- Health risks are similarly accentuated.

This relationship occurs on both international and national scales. For example, in Nicaragua the municipalities affected by Hurricane Mitch were those with the highest levels of poverty, especially in rural areas. Of the 58 poorest municipalities in the country, 40 are located in the provinces which were worst affected by the hurricane.

There is a range of ways of dealing with climatic hazards:

- accepting them and living with the losses
- accepting them but insuring against losses
- avoiding or reducing the hazard by intelligent siting of settlements
- attempting to manage their impacts by:
  - hard management (e.g. dams, dykes)
  - soft management (e.g. land-use changes, such as reforestation)

Drought: El Niño gets the blame

Papua New Guinea seems to be adversely impacted by El Niño events, which cause drought in the country. El Niño occurs when the water in the eastern Pacific is warmer than usual. The opposite (colder than normal water in the eastern Pacific) is called La Niña and this causes heavy rains and flooding in Papua New Guinea.

There was an El Niño event in 1997–98. In Papua New Guinea, severe drought conditions began in mid-1997 and extended into the early months of 1998. By the end of 1997, an estimated 700 000 inhabitants were adversely affected by food shortages, with 40% of the country's rural population suffering severe shortages.

Despite a 6-month relief effort, hundreds died of drought-related causes (food shortages, lack of water and an increase in the incidence of infectious disease). The highland provinces were doubly affected, because the lack of cloud cover produced frost, which also reduced crop output. This was similar to the situation that occurred in the highlands of Papua New Guinea during the 1972–73 El Niño and the intense 1982–83 El Niño. However, El Niño-related climate anomalies were not the only problems that the leaders of Papua New Guinea faced during 1997–98. At least some of the problems were caused by poor food distribution, corruption and neglect of rural regions. Blaming a catastrophe on 'natural' forces is very tempting for governments who might otherwise have to accept some blame themselves.

Exam tip In August 1998, the Chinese government changed its story of blaming El Niño for the devastating floods of 1997. It now believes that the floods were largely caused by deforestation in the Yangtse River's watershed. This is a bold admission — a government taking blame (and responsibility) for human activities, most likely allowed (if not encouraged) by decades of government policy.

Glaciated and periglacial environments offer opportunities and challenges for human activity

Mountainous regions

In most cases, mountainous regions are inaccessible and environmentally fragile. They are frequently marginalised or neglected by political and economic decision making, because of their inaccessibility and their low-population densities, which make them electorally insignificant. Thus they are often poor, peripheral and remote regions.

Not every mountainous region is glaciated and not all glacial erosion or deposition takes place in mountains. Major physical constraints (challenges) exist in most mountainous regions, whether glaciated or not, including:

- relatively more extreme climatic parameters with the consequent reduction in the growing season
- steepness of slopes
- thin soils
- inaccessibility and consequent long travel times

To this can be added distinctive human challenges:

- low population density, leading to shortage of skills and labour
- low electoral importance, leading to neglect and remoteness from the centre or core
- vulnerability to economic change

Those mountain regions that have been glaciated may have particularly restrictive physical environments, given that over-deepening of river valleys and stripping of topsoil make them even more inaccessible, increase slope angle and reduce the carrying capacity through further limitations on the availability of fertile soil. In extreme cases, such as in parts of Norway, communication between communities was, until recently, only possible by boat.

These remote rural societies are characterised by:

- relatively few people
- dependence on natural resources
- limited educational opportunities after secondary school
- limited job availability and opportunities for skilled and educated labour
- the absence of urban commodities, such as restaurants, theatres and sports centres

Consequently, many mountainous regions, such as those of Europe, have been particularly exposed to population decline and a subsequent loss in vitality as soon as they become integrated into a national economy. There is some evidence that those furthest from the core (e.g. southern Italy) have suffered greater decline than those closer to the economic centre of Europe (e.g. Switzerland).

Mountains are home to about 10% of the global population. Nearly 30% of this population depends directly on the resources derived from mountain regions. Functionally, mountains play a critical role in the environment and economic process of the planet. The economic opportunities include forestry, mineral extraction, power generation through hydro-electric schemes, livestock rearing, tourism and recreation.

Mineral extraction in the Andes

The Andes stretch for 7500 km along the western edge of South America, from the equator to Tierra del Fuego. As a result, they contain the most extreme variations in landscape, vegetation and climate of any mountain group in the world. The central Andes are characterised by large high plateaux above 3500 m known as **puna** or **altiplano**, which are the most densely populated areas of the range. In Peru, 50% of the population live in the mountains, 33% in the puna. Residents of these high plateaux grow frost-resistant crops (e.g. potatoes) and, in common with mountain populations all around the world, are heavily dependent on the grazing of hardy animals. In Peru these are llamas, alpacas and sheep. The central Andes were also the heartland of the highly sophisticated Inca empire and have therefore become a focus for tourist activity.

In the area around Cerro de Pasco, the traditional herding lifestyle has been eroded by the introduction of mining. Although this has brought employment and some infrastructure to the region, it has also caused environmental problems, including:

- waste from the mines seeping into the water supply
- pollution of springs that feed the meadows
- destruction of ecosystems in the lakes
- atmospheric pollution
- deterioration of the health of people and livestock

Exam tip Peru is better known in Europe for its growing tourist industry, which is largely based in the mountains. There are conflicts between the development of a tourist industry built around Inca culture and the extraction industries described here.

Iceland

Icelanders have long been dependent on a harsh environment for their survival. The fisheries surrounding Iceland supply 80% of the country's export earnings, bringing wealth to many and generating the capital to drive Iceland's service economy, which has recently developed a distinctive quaternary sector specialising in tourist-related information and exploiting its knowledge of geothermal power. However, fishing is not without its costs. In one small town of 5000 inhabitants on Haemay Island, 500 fishermen have lost their lives since 1860.

The glacial environment of Iceland has provided both a challenge and, more recently, opportunities. The development of the glaciers, especially Vatnajökull and Myrdalsjökull, as tourist locations has also led to a spin-off quaternary industry which is largely based in Reykjavik and specialises in off-road adventure and snowmobile holidays.

Tourism has begun to have an impact. The countryside is both beautiful and dramatic and Icelandic society has an extraordinary history of isolation, in which a literary, story-telling culture has developed. Although the tourist numbers will never rival those of the Alps (partly because of Iceland's cold, wet summers), in proportion to the total Icelandic population the impact of tourists is significant.

Cultural changes and exposure to outside influences have led to younger Icelanders becoming more materialistic (as has happened in parts of the world from the west of Ireland to the Andes), while Reykjavik, the capital, has grown from a small village with 1200 people in 1850 to a town with more than 50% of the country's population by 1990.

Icelandic tourism is not well organised; limited accommodation and a rather repetitive cuisine are drawbacks. Nevertheless, the number of tourists has grown dramatically over the last 20 years and, as is common with tourism, a few localities receive concentrated attention. One of these is the Skaftafell National Park:

- Skaftafell is a small community close to the 2119 m summit of Öraefajökull, looking out across the outwash plains and volcanoes.
- It dates back to the earliest settlements in Iceland and has been farmed by the same family since 1400.
- Until the 1950s, Skaftafell could only be reached on horseback across dangerous glacier meltwater rivers. As a consequence, visitors were few.
- In 1969, with help from the WWF, the Icelandic government bought the farms and made Skaftafell the centre of the country's first National Park.
- In 1974, the river was bridged and Skaftafell became accessible from Reykjavik by bus. A visitors' centre and camp site were open by the time the road was completed.
- The first year (1974) saw 13 000 overnight stays. This increased steadily, exceeding 24 000 by 1985. An increasing proportion of visitors were from overseas; foreigners exceeded 50% in 1987.

This growth of interest in Skaftafell was demonstrated by a 1987 hotel association questionnaire, which indicated that it was the most popular destination in Iceland.

There are two important themes when considering the growth of tourism at Skaftafell:

- visitor impact
- management policy

The landscape is the main attraction. Despite the fact that visitor numbers are quite modest, the landscape is very fragile. Short walks bring tourists to dramatic glacier views with ice avalanches. Thus, the physical impact on fragile ecosystems is significant and spreading. While the government has so far resisted pressure to permit park entry by four-wheel drive vehicles, pressure continues to rise as Iceland becomes both more affluent and more dependent on tourist revenue.

The second theme relates to the government's attempt to restore the natural vegetation by eliminating sheep grazing from the surrounding hill and mountain slopes. (Sheep are not 'native' to Iceland.) As a result of this policy, the farms no longer operate. The policy is based upon the United States National Park ideology, which assumes incompatibility between 'natural' mountain landscape and human occupation. This is in marked contrast to the UK tradition of National Parks embracing human occupation as a key element in the formation of landscape. Without sheep, Icelanders would have died out during the Little Ice Age 200 years ago, as their cousins did in Greenland.

This raises questions about our understanding of 'natural' landscapes and the role of humans in their creation.

Exam tip This is a very useful example of the complexity of the interface between the 'natural' landscape and the man-made landscape. Synoptic geography often sets up the 'physical' environment and the 'human' environment as though they are mutually exclusive and easily determined categories. This is not the case if we accept the fact that humans are part of the biosphere.

Living with permafrost

Permafrost underlies an estimated 20–25% of the world's land surface; it occurs in more than 50% of Russia and Canada, 82% of Alaska and 20% of China. Permafrost in northern Siberia is 1600 m thick; it is 650 m thick in northern Alaska.

The active surface layer of permafrost thaws every summer and freezes in winter. A frozen sub-layer prevents the water soaking into the ground beneath. The active layer is vulnerable to environmental damage. For example, tracks from a passing vehicle will tear up the fragile, insulating tundra, allowing the soil to thaw into scars that may remain for hundreds of years.

Permafrost regions of the planet are cold, remote and frequently inaccessible. Almost all have supported indigenous peoples (e.g. the Inuits) who have survived despite the permafrost, rather than because of it. In recent years, some of these regions have been more closely integrated into the global economy, sometimes with a complex set of impacts on the landscape and the people.

As development pressures increase in arctic and subarctic areas, planning approaches and techniques do not always take into account the environmental impacts of development, especially in poorer regions such as Siberia.

It is becoming increasingly recognised that the terrain around building sites in the Arctic should be disturbed as little as possible. The impacts of development on permafrost soils occur very slowly over long periods of time. It may be too early to tell how well we have adapted our land-use practices to the arctic lands. Development during the 1970s and 1980s in Alaska, which occurred as a result of the oil boom, may not be sustainable over the long term.

When developing housing or supporting infrastructure, there are several general approaches to dealing with permafrost:

- Ignore it — if there is virtually no water in the soil, thawing of the permafrost will not significantly affect its bearing strength.
- Thaw it — this can be done by removing vegetation. Often, peat and other permafrost-susceptible layers are dug out of the building site and replaced with gravel or sand. Such an approach is more appropriate for the discontinuous zone of permafrost, where it is thinner and unlikely to refreeze after thawing. (Soil replacement has been carried out extensively in Fairbanks, Alaska.)
- Prevent it from thawing — the best approach in the continuous zone. There are several ways in which this can be accomplished:
  - Ventilation allows circulation of air between the bottom of the structure and the soil surface. Gravel pads fitted with ventilation ducts allow this. Insulating matting is sometimes used in conjunction with the pads.
  - More commonly, piles are used to raise the building several feet above the ground. They are usually driven down twice the thickness of the active layer, which avoids the problem of frost-heaving. The pile placements are often surrounded with material that readily freezes the piles in place.
  - On airport runways and other dark surfaces, white paint has been used to reflect solar energy that would otherwise be transmitted down to the soil and cause thawing.
  - The use of coarse gravel roadbeds helps stop water moving upwards under roadways and forming ice lenses and frost heave.
  - The supply of utilities to buildings on permafrost is problematic because the pipes for water and sewers might thaw the soil (or might themselves freeze). Raising the pipes on low pilings is one common solution.

There is increasing concern that global warming will cause thawing of vast areas of permafrost. If this does occur, it will have serious implications for human settlement. Stable soils may become more prone to subsidence. There may be an increase in solifluction and landslides. In several communities in the interior of Alaska, general thawing of the permafrost has been blamed for widespread undermining of buildings and roads. A larger issue, related to the thawing of permafrost, is the potential release of gases from the decomposition of now frozen organic soils. These gases could exacerbate global warming.

Ecosystems offer opportunities and challenges for human activity

The Serengeti National Park

The Serengeti National Park is one of the best-known game reserves in Africa. The herds of ungulates and associated predators make it one of the most complex ecosystems in Africa. The park, in combination with the adjacent Ngorongoro Conservation Area and Maasai Mara National Park, is sufficiently large to ensure survival of the savanna ecosystem.

Management issues in the Serengeti

- The human population to the west of the park has expanded rapidly over the past 30 years; wildlife and livestock populations have also grown and demand for land is high.
- Grazing land is becoming scarce, as pastureland is converted into cropland.
- Local people are vulnerable to external development and large-scale agricultural schemes, which do not benefit local communities.
- Open land ownership has resulted in local people over-exploiting common resources.
- Agricultural encroachments have appeared on park boundaries and former subsistence poaching has now become large scale and commercial.
- An estimated 200 000 animals are killed annually, resulting in large decreases in the numbers of some species.
- The increased demand for meat has been partly driven by the growing local population and in-migration, as wildlife and fuel wood are depleted elsewhere.
- The need for bushmeat has also been exacerbated by the relatively low contribution tourism has made to the local economy.
- At one time, elephants did not inhabit the Serengeti. However, cultivation and settlement outside the park have resulted in a change in distribution.
- The combination of elephants, uncontrolled fires, and subsequent browsing and stunting of regrowth by giraffe, has caused a decline in woodlands.
- Approximately 30 000 domestic dogs live in the area, most of which are not vaccinated, thus creating a large reservoir for disease.

Exam tip Much of this raises the issue of conflict between communities who live and survive in areas that are of international 'environmental' significance and the governments and development lobbies that wish to exploit them differently.

In 1951, the original boundary of the National Park included land to the south and east of the present park and the Ngorongoro Highlands. **Pastoralism** and cultivation by the Maasai were allowed to continue until 1954, when it was felt that this was incompatible with resource conservation. The park was divided into the present-day Serengeti National Park and the Ngorongoro Conservation Area. The National Park was set aside strictly for wildlife conservation and tourism, with restricted human access. Throughout the 1980s, this **preservationist approach** to protected area management slowly changed to a **conservation and development**

programme. The overall goal is to change the management and use of the Serengeti from the traditional approach, which has excluded and alienated local communities, to one in which human development in the region is reconciled with natural resource conservation.

- It has been recognised that wildlife is an important economic resource for rural communities around the park.
- It is hoped that creating schemes whereby local communities are given legal rights to manage the wildlife around their villages will prevent the present illegal and unsustainable levels of wildlife poaching from the park.
- Areas suitable for development as buffer zones to the park have been identified, where wildlife can be managed by the local people and village Wildlife Committees can supervise conservation activities.
- The Serengeti Regional Conservation Strategy also includes programmes to stabilise land use, and plans to channel more money earned from tourist activities within the park back into the community.
- The park administration works with the village authorities to resettle encroachers and re-mark the boundary.

Community management of forest resources

- Community-based forest management involves and benefits the local community.
- Balancing economic, social and environmental factors in the management of forest resources has emerged as one of the key challenges in natural resource management. Major global trends such as increasing corporate control, economic globalisation, growing awareness of environmental issues and stronger community organisations are changing the environment in which decisions concerning natural resource management are being made.
- Among the responses to these trends is the emergence of initiatives supporting local forest management as a viable alternative to centralised control.
- Throughout the world, a large number of forestry projects with participatory local forest management or community forestry components are being implemented, initiated or planned.
- Community-based forest management is founded on the enjoyment of the benefits of the local forest resource. These benefits are not just monetary; neither are they derived exclusively from timber production. They include cultural, spiritual, social, medicinal, ecological, recreational, aesthetic and economic values. Community-based forest management presents an opportunity for the interests and values of local citizens to be reflected in a range of diverse approaches to forest use.

All community-based forest management initiatives:

- support the control, management and use of forest and timber resources by local communities
- respect the social, economic and cultural relationships between people and forests
- involve a decentralised and participatory approach to forest management, which assumes that the best stewards of the world's forests are the populations living in and around them

Community-based forest management projects vary in their objectives and may include such initiatives as the sustainable management of large forest tracts, reforestation and plantations.

Soil erosion

All systems can be evaluated in terms of:

- stability — the ability of a system to return to its previous 'equilibrium' state after temporary disturbance
- resilience — the capacity of a system to absorb change without significantly altering the community composition
- spatial significance (scale)
- human and geological time scales

	Water erosion	Wind erosion	Soil structure decline
Types	• Raindrop splash Sheetwash (rainwash) — overland flow • Rill and gully erosion • Piping and tunnelling — subsurface flow • Bank erosion and river bed scour	—	—
Controlling factors	• Rainfall erosivity (intensity, duration) • Soil erodibility (texture, structure, organic content) • Gradient • Type of land surface cover (vegetation, crusts, stones) • Density of land surface cover • Land management practices (present and past)	• Soil erodibility (texture, structure, organic matter content, moisture content) • Type and density of land surface cover • Land management practices (e.g. overgrazing) • Meteorological conditions (wind speed, dryness)	• Soil characteristics (binding agents, clay content and type, organic matter content, soluble and exchangeable cations) • Rainfall characteristics (intensity) • Land surface cover (vegetation) • Land management practices (machinery, animals)
Consequences	• Topsoil and (sometimes) subsoil loss • Loss of nutrients and organic matter • Downslope and downstream siltation • Lowering of the water table • Damage to infrastructure	• Topsoil loss • Loss of nutrients and organic matter • Reduced visibility • Contamination of water bodies • Burying of cropland and infrastructure, especially fences, by wind drifts	• Compacted upper subsoil • Discontinuous pores • Reduced porosity • Increased soil strength

- change:
  - long term (irreversible or permanent change in terms of human life time, i.e. it takes more than 50 years to fix)
  - short term (reversible or temporary change, i.e. it can be readily fixed in time frames of the order of 5–10 years)
- the magnitude and frequency of events or activities:
  - low magnitude/high frequency versus high magnitude/low frequency (which does the most geomorphological work?)
  - important in deciding management strategies (what is the risk that we are prepared to underwrite, both financially and as a community?)

Erosion of soil can be caused by:

- water — entrainment, transport and (consequently) deposition of fine-grained materials (organic and mineral) by water
- wind — entrainment, transport and (consequently) deposition of fine-grained materials (organic and mineral) by wind moving over a surface
- decline in soil structure — reduction in continuity and distribution of soil pores caused by soil manipulation (usually repeated use of machinery such as tractors and ploughs)

Summary of impact

- Soil erosion is a huge problem. It has been estimated that, globally, 3 million km^2 (an area the size of western Europe) of arable land have been strongly degraded over the past 100 years. Another 9 million km^2 have been moderately degraded and a further 1.5 million km^2 may be degraded in the next 20 years, unless changes are made.
- Land degradation rates are exceeding the opening of new lands for agriculture. Therefore, there is a net loss of land for food production.
- Soil formation occurs over long geological time scales and averages less than 0.1 mm yr^{-1}. This means that topsoil loss exceeds replacement by a factor of at least 1000.

Management objectives are:

- to minimise disturbance
- to retain as much soil as possible on site
- to promote stability in the long-term change in farming practices — this may mean a reduction in farming intensity

Exam tip This is a difficult issue. If arable farmland is being lost through soil erosion, then the only routes to greater food production for a growing global population are:

- to increase the yield from the land currently being farmed, which would normally be achieved by adopting at least some of the farming practices that caused the problem in the first place
- to change the cultural preference in most MEDCs away from a diet with a high meat content

Synoptic links from Unit 5

Industrialisation and de-industrialisation impact on the environment

The natural environment and physical factors clearly have some impact on the choice of industrial location, although this varies from industry to industry.

The natural environment is a broad term that might embrace anything from the general attractiveness of the landscape to the climate. Physical factors involve small-scale site elements that influence the choice of location for individual plants or factories.

Site factors include:

- availability of flat land
- ability to expand
- accessibility
- water supply
- ability to dispose of waste

Exam tip Remember that 'industry' is just another word for work and is interchangeable with economic activity, covering any area of employment from primary to quaternary.

The relationship between the physical environment and industry is particularly obvious in regions of the world that have industrialised quickly and have therefore developed a heavy-industry base built around potentially polluting industries such as chemicals, iron and steel, and power production. These areas frequently mirror the lack of concern about the environment shown in the UK during the Industrial Revolution. Among the most notorious of these 'late developers' are countries that formerly belonged to the Warsaw Pact and were pushed into rapid development by their Russian advisers.

Poland

Economy and industry

Despite the fall of the Soviet Union and the building of a capitalist economy in the former eastern bloc countries, large-scale industry in Poland remains mainly in state hands. Since 1990, inflation has declined. Manufacturing industry accounts for 25% of total employment. In the agri-food sector, production is rising rapidly and many of Poland's largest companies are in the food industry. The chemical industry consists mainly of large state companies with some private enterprises. There are 23 steel mills in Poland. Production has dropped since 1986, but has now stabilised. There are many environmental problems connected with the steel industry. Modernisation programmes are planned, but it will take time to solve the technical, commercial and management deficiencies.

Environment

The environmental situation has improved since 1990 because of a decline in heavy industry and increased government concerns about environmental issues. When the economy started to improve, industrial pollution did not rise at the same rate because of a large investment programme, industrial restructuring and the incentive effect of the economic strategies developed after 1989.

Poland still has severe environmental problems. Acid rain has taken its toll on Polish forests and the health of the people is threatened by large amounts of sulphur dioxide, nitrogen oxides, carbon dioxide, dust particulates, heavy metals (lead, cadmium, arsenic, mercury) and carcinogenic hydrocarbons escaping into the atmosphere. The Polish energy sector is a major source of pollutants because it still relies on coal as its primary fuel source.

During the 1980s, Poland's Katowice district, which is part of the Silesia region and makes up 2.1% of the country's area, accounted for as much as 20–25% of the emissions of sulphur dioxide, nitrogen oxides and dust. In the region now known as 'the black triangle', home to the largest basin of brown coal in Europe, approximately 200 million tonnes of coal were produced each year, leading to annual emissions of 3 million tonnes of sulphur dioxide and 1 million tonnes of nitrogen oxides.

Environmental pollution in Silesia resulted from years of high industrial activity concentrated within a relatively small area. Emission of excessive amounts of pollutants resulted in severe acid rain, practically destroying the mountain forests and acidifying the soils in the Karkonosze and the Izerskie Mountains. As a result of the poor air quality, the death rate for men in Katowice between the ages of 30 and 59 exceeds the national average by 40%, children are usually born underweight, and the occurrence of birth defects in the region is up to 60% more common than Poland's average.

It is expected that the recent accession to the OECD and membership of the EU will provide a stimulus for improvements in pollution, specifically in the area of hazardous waste management. Since 1989, significant resources have been made available for upgrading 300 wastewater treatment plants. However, further investments in this sector are needed. In 1990, the government required power plants to initiate action for an approximate 30% reduction in sulphur dioxide, nitrogen dioxide and dust levels by 1997. For plants put into operation after the ordinance took effect, the permitted levels are much lower. An environmental policy was adopted in 1991, and in 1995 a review of policy implementation was published, setting detailed targets to the year 2000. By utilising environmental fees and fines, Poland has been quite successful in obtaining financial resources to reduce industrial and water pollution.

Exam tip Pollution of the environment is costly and many of these costs fall on people not responsible for the original damage. These are external costs and in most economic systems companies are not keen to pay for this sort of damage. In other words, there is often the need for governments to intervene to insist that companies either do not pollute or, if it is really unavoidable, pay for some of the damage done — 'internalising the externalities'. This is especially difficult if the externalities are exported beyond national boundaries, as with acid rain.

The Polish example also illustrates how what are frequently perceived as national problems are, in reality, much more localised. It is another case where care is needed before blaming the nation.

Generation of waste

Rising incomes and economic growth favouring domestic consumption are both likely to increase waste. For some 20 years, industrialised countries have been producing increasing amounts of rubbish that has to be disposed of.

- In the USA, waste generation stands at 870 kg per person each year, or 2.5 kg a day.
- In 1997, about 64% of global waste was put into landfill sites, 18% incinerated and 18% recycled.
- For every job dumping waste in a landfill site, recycling could create ten jobs. Use of waste as raw materials would also reduce our demand for new resources.
- Babies born within 3 km of landfill sites taking hazardous waste have an increased risk of chromosomal abnormalities and other birth defects.
- Recycling aluminium can bring energy savings of up to 95%. It also reduces emissions of greenhouse gases by 95% compared with aluminium production from ore.
- Although the productive use of waste has increased in industrialised countries, it is still not sufficient to reverse the trend of rising volumes requiring disposal.
- OECD forecasts predicted that production of municipal waste (estimated at 540 million tonnes in 1997) would increase by 43% between 1997 and 2020.
- In an attempt to slow down this development, the EU has issued many directives designed to encourage the productive use of waste of all kinds, from the largest (e.g. vehicles and electrical goods) to the smallest (e.g. batteries and packaging).

Exam tip The short-term benefits of landfill as a means of waste disposal may be outweighed by the long-term costs for which we do not yet have a complete picture. Long-term health problems arising from methane emissions, housing subsidence and groundwater toxicity are among the best documented effects.

Are the French setting the trends?

France was one of the first European countries to take the management of its waste seriously and after 10 years the picture is generally encouraging.

About 80% of French people are worried about the environment and most are quite prepared to sort their household waste. According to the latest statistics, annual production of waste (excluding waste soil and rock) in France is estimated at 600 million tonnes, most of it consisting of agricultural waste (350 million tonnes) and building-site waste (110 million tonnes).

Every French person throws away an average of over a kilo of waste material each day. In 2001, among European countries, France was second only to Germany in terms of sorting rubbish. France processes 1.7 million tonnes of household packaging each year in 250 approved sorting centres. The officially approved waste-management body has set itself the target of recycling 65% of household packaging.

Exam tip In recent years, in the wealthiest countries, there has been a shift away from relaxed attitudes to waste management. These changing values have been reflected in the greater prominence afforded to 'green' issues by politicians. In both France and Germany, political advances made by various green parties have more or less pushed mainstream political parties into action.

Do MEDCs export their rubbish?

Between 1994 and 1996, a German company sent 95 000 tonnes of household rubbish to Pyongyang, North Korea. The North Korean workers who processed the waste could have been affected by fumes and toxins released during the recycling process. It may be that the health of the workforce is not a primary consideration in North Korea and that this is one possible reason why it is cheaper to send waste many thousands of kilometres for recycling.

This story was very emotive for Germans who saw themselves as world leaders in waste recycling. The German spokesman for Greenpeace commented that 'Germany was the world master in exporting rubbish overseas' and went on to list over 30 countries, including China, Indonesia, Pakistan, Vietnam and the Philippines, to which German companies made 'legal or illegal' rubbish shipments.

Environmentalism

Concern about the environment is not new. However, it is largely a product of industrialisation and occasionally includes nostalgia about a pre-industrial world. Concern has grown alongside high mass consumption and is seen by critics as a hypocritical indulgence. The idea of stopping environmental destruction is rather easier for those who have achieved material wealth than for people who are still striving for developmental goals. Therefore, appropriate questions might be:

- Who benefits most from slowing down the rate of deforestation in the Amazon?
- Who benefited most from the deforestation of Europe?
- Does the fact that Bengal tigers do not threaten the life or livelihood of any Europeans influence our attitude towards them?
- Did bears and wolves threaten the livelihoods of any northern Europeans? What did they do about it?
- What gives us the right to lecture poorer societies about the environment?

Exam tip There is no one 'correct' attitude towards nature, any more than there is one universally accepted idea of what nature is. Some people include human beings as an integral part of nature, thus exonerating us from any blame; others place 'man' and 'nature' in opposition.

The view that the natural world is there to be exploited in the pursuit of personal gain has dominated Western culture until recently. In the history of environmentalism in Britain, different conceptions of 'nature' have been seen to affect both values and policy. Hill walkers, bird watchers, preservationists and green-spacers have all claimed to know what 'nature' really is, and have had varying degrees of success in including their differing visions in planning arrangements and statutory schemes.

There are many questions to consider; for instance:

- Which system, which 'nature', is being protected?
- Are humans in or out of the 'natural' world?
- In environmental terms, is 'nature' some imaginary world without the impact of human history, without landscapes transformed, species eradicated and plant varieties cultivated?
- Is it 'nature as scenery'—the world with the human interventions we like, whether they be hedgerows, dry-stone walls or the bleak beauty of a deforested and depopulated Scottish moor?

The dominant scientific view about the environment makes gloomy reading. Environmental problems have gone from bad to worse in the past 50 years:

- 15–20% of all species have already been lost, threatening the fifth great extinction (the last being the dinosaurs). Bird and mammal species are disappearing at an estimated 100–1000 times the rate at which extinctions occur naturally.
- Tropical deforestation has occurred at a rate of around a hectare every 2.5 seconds. About 100 000 km^2 are made barren each year by desertification.
- Growing energy use has led to a 2–3°C rise in mid-latitude temperatures, and to significant changes in rainfall patterns, over the past 100 years.
- Half of the world's mangroves and wetlands have been destroyed.
- Industry and agriculture are fixing nitrogen at rates exceeding nature. Among the consequences of the resulting over-fertilisation are 50 dead zones in the oceans.
- In 1960, 5% of marine fisheries were either fished to capacity or over-fished. Today, 70% are in this condition.

Governments have not only failed to reverse these trend, but; they have laid a poor foundation for future progress. Many years of international environmental negotiations have had disappointing results. What has been agreed upon, for example, in the conventions on climate, desertification and biodiversity is sound enough, but most of it is simply advisory. Governments sign up to protocols or agreements that they support in principle, but then fail to work vigorously towards their implementation.

The agreements were forged with procedures that gave maximum leverage to countries with an interest in thwarting international action. The USA successfully weakened the Kyoto Protocol; Brazil has worked to keep a forest convention at bay; Japan and other major fishing countries watered down the international marine fisheries agreement.

There is no international consensus on environmental protection. Indeed, there is no consensus within countries between different interest groups.

Rapid change has created pressure on rural–urban interdependence

China's air quality

Official statistics show that in 1999, only eight of China's 47 major cities satisfied the state environmental requirements for both air and groundwater quality. Twenty-eight cities met the environmental protection requirements for groundwater quality but not for air quality. Fifteen cities, including Beijing, failed to meet discharge requirements for total suspended particles (TSP), sulphur dioxide and nitrogen oxide. All of these cities have experienced recent, rapid population growth and industrialisation as China has modernised.

Of 29 cities that failed to meet the state TSP discharge requirement, Lanzhou was the most polluted, with a TSP level 2.5 times higher than the state requirement. Lanzhou has come up with a radical solution — demolishing a mountain to let in some fresh air. This scheme is based on the theory that the surrounding mountains block the movement of air to the city, which is in a natural depression, and cause a build-up of pollutants.

The solution has been controversial — popular with developers but not with the local people who have expressed doubts about whether it will work. There have also been protests from people whose ancestors are buried in tombs on the hill. Water is being used to erode the mountain; 10 000 gallons a day are pumped from the Yellow River to the summit. The water is then allowed to flow down a zigzag path as workers shovel soil into the flow. This is the cheapest way to shift so much material.

China's water quality

Every year, large amounts of pollutants are dumped into China's water bodies from agricultural, domestic and industrial sources (see Figure 4).

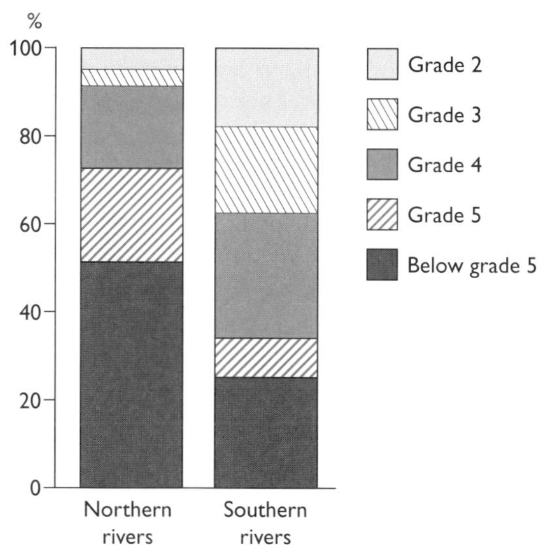

Figure 4 Water quality of 135 urban river sections in China (grades 4 and 5 are deemed unsuitable for direct human contact)

Agriculture

China is the world's largest consumer of synthetic nitrogen fertilisers. These are used to increase agricultural yield to feed the huge and growing population. As a result, pollution is widespread in China's rivers and lakes. This has worsened in recent years, with the pollution adjacent to industrially developed cities and towns being particularly severe.

Industrial wastewater

In 1995, only 77% of industrial wastewater received any treatment and nearly 50% failed to meet government standards. Industrial discharges usually contain a range of toxic pollutants such as petroleum, cyanide, arsenic and heavy metals. This is difficult to control because of China's widely scattered distribution of industry in a very large country. Since pursuit of economic benefits is China's first goal, local authorities are also reluctant to tighten pollution controls.

Domestic waste

Treatment of domestic sewage is even less advanced. In 1995, China had only 100 modern wastewater treatment plants. Beijing had only one secondary sewage treatment plant, with a capacity of 500 000 tonnes, which was inadequate.

> **Exam tip** The push for rapid development has come at the expense of a clean environment. Production would have higher costs and be less competitive in world markets if pollution controls were in place and rigorously applied.

Smog

Smog forms when pollutants released from petrol- and diesel-powered vehicles react with heat and sunlight. It can inflame breathing airways, decreasing the working capacity of the lungs. It is particularly harmful to the elderly, children, asthmatics, and people with heart and lung conditions.

Recent studies have linked the tiny particles emitted by diesel engines directly to health problems, including heart attacks and childhood asthma. On average, a car pumps out more than 3 tonnes of carbon dioxide, the foremost greenhouse gas, every year.

Six of the world's smoggiest cities are to benefit from the introduction of fuel-cell powered buses. The 5-year, $60 million programme will provide 40–50 such buses for each of Mexico City, São Paulo, Cairo, New Delhi, Shanghai and Beijing.

A fuel cell powers vehicles by electricity, which it creates by reacting hydrogen with oxygen. The only emission from fuel-cell vehicles is water vapour, so they are significantly cleaner than petrol and diesel vehicles. Fuel-cell technology can help to alleviate health risks and reduce greenhouse gas emissions that contribute to global warming.

Sustainable tourism criteria

Sustainable tourism seeks to minimise ecological and sociocultural impacts while providing economic benefits to local communities and host countries.

In any scheme, the criteria used to define sustainable tourism should address at least minimum standards in the following aspects (where relevant):

Aspect	Criteria
Overall	• Environmental planning and impact assessment have been undertaken and social, cultural, ecological and economic impacts considered (including cumulative impacts and strategies to limit them) • Environmental management commitment by tourism businesses • Staff training, education, responsibility, knowledge and awareness in environmental, social and cultural management • Mechanisms for monitoring and reporting environmental performance • Accurate, responsible marketing, leading to realistic expectations • Consumer feedback
Social/cultural	• Impacts upon social structures, culture and economy (at both local and national levels) considered • Appropriateness of land acquisition/access processes and land tenure • Measures to protect the integrity of the local community's social structure • Mechanisms to ensure rights and aspirations of local and/or indigenous people are recognised
Ecological	• Appropriateness of location and sense of place • Biodiversity conservation and integrity of ecosystem processes • Site disturbance, landscaping and rehabilitation • Drainage, soils and storm water management • Sustainability of energy supply and minimisation of use • Sustainability of water supply and minimisation of use • Sustainability of wastewater treatment and disposal • Noise and air quality (including greenhouse emissions) • Waste minimisation and sustainability of disposal • Visual impact and light • Sustainability of materials and supplies (e.g. recyclable and recycled materials, locally produced, certified timber products) • Environmental impacts of activities
Economic	• Requirements for ethical business practice • Mechanisms to ensure labour arrangements and industrial relations procedures are not exploitative, and conform to local laws and international labour standards (whichever are higher) • Mechanisms to ensure negative economic impacts on local communities are minimised and preferably that there are substantial economic benefits to local communities • Requirements to ensure contributions to the development or maintenance of local community infrastructure

The world is increasingly interdependent

The definition of development

Development is a multidimensional process involving social, economic, political and cultural phenomena, in which the ultimate goal is to improve living standards.

In almost all attempts to define development, the following are common objectives:

- to increase the availability and widen the distribution of basic life-sustaining goods
- to raise the standard of living, including, in addition to higher incomes, the provision of shelter, food, education and employment
- to increase the economic and social choices available to individuals and nations

This is uncontroversial, although different priorities are often given to these three objectives and there is some considerable disagreement about the detail. For example, the nature of 'social choice' may very well be disputed between the protagonists in the debate about abortion. However, the real disagreements begin when the three main ideologies that dominate this subject are reviewed:

- Liberalism assumes that politics and economics exist in separate spheres.
- Nationalism assumes and advocates the primacy of politics over economics.
- Marxism holds that economics drives politics.

These views are not readily compatible — one cannot easily take a little from each school of thought. Their significance is that the preferred ideology clearly influences the chosen **route to development**. Thus for all practical purposes, the policies adopted within a country by the government, and the acceptance of those policies by the citizens, are determined by ideology.

Very few dispute the factual accuracy of the increasing disparity in world income shown in the following table:

World income inequality	1960	1970	1980	1989	1998
20% 'low'	2.3%	2.3%	1.7%	1.4%	1.2%
60% 'middle'	27.5%	23.6%	22.0%	15.9%	9.8%
20% 'high'	70.2%	73.9%	76.3%	82.7%	89.0%
Gini (income inequality) coefficient	0.54	0.57	0.60	0.65	0.70

However, the interpretation of these disparities varies according to the ideological position held.

The liberal view:

- The world is a much richer place, so absolute poverty has decreased.
- Wealth has to be created by the rich before it can trickle down to the poor.
- The speed of this trickle-down has not been helped by misguided opposition to globalisation.
- There is plenty of evidence of successful narrowing of the 'gap', e.g. Taiwan.

The nationalist view:

- There is some validity in these data because countries have been sucked into a world system, which has impoverished them.
- States need to be able to develop their own industrial base or they risk being trapped by declining terms of trade and increasing dependency on manufactured goods from richer countries — hence the widening gap.

The Marxist view:

- There are poor people in every country and they are getting poorer — look at average wage rates in the USA.
- The nation state is not a useful model for analysis. There is no 'United Kingdom' because there are different classes who are fundamentally opposed to one another.
- The disparity of income is an inevitable part of advanced capitalism and will lead to its downfall.

Who benefits from development?

In many developing countries, the social system is characterised by stratification based not only on gender, but also on class. Rural Bangladesh presents an especially pronounced social hierarchy.

- The economic and political power is rooted primarily in land ownership.
- The uppermost class, possessing 2 hectares or more of land, accounts for only about 8% of all rural households, but controls almost 48% of all the cultivatable land.
- Lowest in the scale are the 50% comprising marginal landowners and landless people, who hold only about 3.7% of the total land. Lacking formal education and any kind of resources, they enjoy scant social prestige. Most earn their living as daily workers and represent an enormous oversupply of labour, so they are locked into dependence on the rural elite.
- The socially and economically privileged wield political influence in addition to economic power, and control whatever development aid comes to the rural areas.
- In bilateral projects between foreign donors and non-governmental organisations, it is likely that those who have more influence than the poor will siphon off funds.
- To keep the money flowing, when applying for funds many organisations are quick to adopt the latest 'fad' in development cooperation, from 'sustainable development' to 'empowerment of women' and 'participation of target groups'.

Exam tip This sheds a rather different light on the oft-argued position that 'the money never goes to the people who need it'. This attitude is usually a criticism of aid agencies and the (often false) supposition that high administrative costs siphon off large quantities of money before it ever reaches the country concerned.

Sustainability

The concept of 'sustainable development' is not new, although the term itself is much more recent. The apparent tension between population growth and the natural environment was certainly known to Herodotus, writing in the fifth century BC. The term entered common usage following the publication of the Brundtland Report in 1987. This commission also generated the best-known definition of the concept — 'to meet the needs of the present without compromising the ability of future generations to meet their own needs'. But what are these 'needs'?

Economic needs include:

- access to an adequate livelihood or productive assets
- economic security when unemployed, ill or otherwise unable to secure a livelihood.

Social, cultural and health needs include:

- shelter that is healthy, safe, affordable and secure
- access to basic healthcare, education and transport
- protection from environmental hazards

Political needs include:

- freedom to participate in national and local politics in a broad framework that ensures respect for civil and political rights
- the implementation of environmental legislation

Exam tip A universally accepted definition does not exist for many basic concepts used by society, even for those that concern our wellbeing. Sustainable development, without a commonly accepted definition, appeals to virtually all groups who choose to participate in the environmental debate because they can simply feed in to the definition their version of 'adequate livelihood' or 'economic security'. Under such conditions, being 'pro' sustainable development entails no risk or commitment to a specific set of goals or conditions, since none is agreed upon. Thus sustainable development has become an article of faith that is often used but seldom explained.

In broad terms, the concept of sustainable development encompasses:

- help for the very poor, because they are left with no option other than to destroy their environment
- the idea of self-reliant development, within natural resource constraints
- the idea of cost-effective development using differing economic criteria from the traditional approach; that is to say, development should not degrade environmental quality and it should not reduce productivity in the long term
- issues of health control, appropriate technologies, food self-reliance, clean water and shelter
- the notion that people-centred initiatives are needed; human beings are the resources in the concept

A further complication occurs because of the words themselves:

- **Sustainable** suggests the relationship between people and the carrying capacity of the planet.
- **Development** is, by some interpretations, compatible with economic growth with little or no reference to the natural resources base.

The following quote from the Dag Hammarskjöld Foundation makes clear something of the problem: 'Development is a whole: it is an integral, value-loaded, cultural process; it encompasses the natural environment, social relations, education, production, consumption and wellbeing.'

Arguments against sustainability

One of the best-known critics of sustainability is Wilfred Beckerman. He argues that:

- sustainability is an unnecessary concept — the welfare of future generations is already accounted for since natural capital (the environment) and human capital are infinitely substitutable and the free market will 'protect' natural capital

- economic growth works better than sustainable development programmes in decreasing world poverty
- sustainability outlines a programme of 'impractical, selfish and "fuzzy" requirements to preserve intact the environment as we find it today in all its forms'
- sustainability is ethically unacceptable because it requires us to choose, for example, between directing funds to save a species of beetle or to provide sanitary water for the poor

Questions & Answers

This section of the guide contains five Unit 6-style questions. Question 1 is the most important question in your geography A-level. It carries 50 'raw' marks, which translate into 80 uniform marks, only 10 fewer than the total uniform marks for either Unit 4 or Unit 5. It is a resource-based question; you will see the resource booklet for the first time in the examination hall. Question 1 in this guide is followed by two sample answers of differing standard. Questions 2–5 are essay questions from which you have to choose one. In this guide, each of these is followed by one sample answer. The essay questions carry 25 marks each.

Examiner's comments

Sample answers are interspersed with examiner's comments, which are preceded by the icon *e*. A closing summary is also provided, which indicates the mark the answer would have been awarded. The comments are designed to highlight the strengths and weaknesses of the candidate's answer. The examples provided contain illustrations of typical errors and shortcomings (such as irrelevancy, lack of clarity, lack of focus on the wording of the question or shortage of case-study material) as well as evidence of good practice.

Marks

Each answer is assessed against general and specific criteria and then awarded marks at the appropriate level. An indication of the general criteria is provided for your guidance below:

Level 1	1–5 marks	Little accurate knowledge. Little relevance to the question.
Level 2	6–9 marks	Mainly descriptive. Poorly written. Simplistic cause and effect. Lack of fluency.
Level 3	10–14 marks	Sound description. Limited understanding. Some use of examples or data. Linked sentences.
Level 4	15–19 marks	Accurate knowledge. Sound understanding. Detailed and varied exemplification. Well-organised answer.
Level 5	20–25 marks	Wide-ranging knowledge. Thorough explanation. Detailed exemplification. Concepts applied. Fluently written.

Question 1

The Ogallala aquifer

Study the resources and then answer the question that follows.

Resources

Introduction

Precipitation drops to less than 50 cm per year over much of the western USA. The paradox is that this semi-arid region is the source of much US produce and grain crops. Kansas, the wheat state, is too dry to produce wheat unless water is provided by irrigation. Irrigation waters for many of the Great Plains states (from South Dakota to Texas) are taken from a single, massive aquifer, the High Plains or Ogallala aquifer.

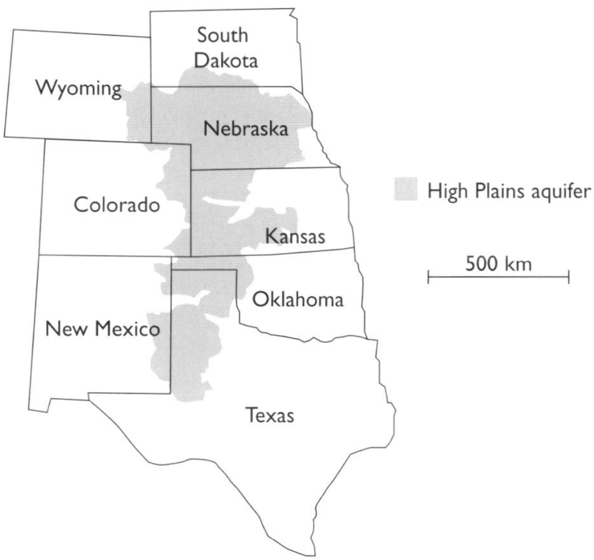

This aquifer underlies much of the Great Plains, including parts of South Dakota, Nebraska, Wyoming, Colorado, Kansas, Oklahoma, New Mexico and Texas

The Ogallala aquifer has been a source for irrigation water since the early 1900s. Approximately 170 000 wells draw water from the aquifer which has brought prosperity to an area described by Major Stephen Long in 1819 as 'almost wholly unfit for cultivation and...uninhabited by people depending upon agriculture for their subsistence'. The aquifer covers an area of 480 000 square kilometres, providing water for the largest area of irrigation-sustained cropland in the world. The equivalent of the entire flow of the Colorado River is taken from the aquifer every year. The level of the underground water in the aquifer is presently dropping at a rate of about 10 feet a year. This means that by 2045, or thereabouts, the whole system will be dry.

Item 1

State	1987–88	1988–89	1989–90	1990–91	1991–92	1992–93
Colorado	+0.11	–0.59	–0.62	–0.48	–0.20	–0.11
Kansas	+0.08	–1.70	–0.24	–0.72	–1.13	+0.50
Nebraska	+0.12	–0.83	–0.59	–0.32	–0.47	+0.32
New Mexico	+0.15	+0.10	–0.29	–0.70	–0.33	–0.81
Oklahoma	+0.80	–0.19	–0.27	–0.04	–0.43	+0.10
South Dakota	–0.08	+0.01	–0.63	+0.45	+0.08	+0.04
Texas	+0.83	+0.16	–1.15	–0.70	–0.61	+0.25
Wyoming	–	–0.61	–0.93	–0.06	+0.11	–0.43
Average	+0.28	–0.65	–0.63	–0.42	–0.55	+0.21

State	1993–94	1994–95	1995–96	1996–97	1997–98	1998–99
Colorado	–0.13	–0.72	–0.12	+0.15	–0.30	–0.24
Kansas	+0.55	–1.20	–0.50	+0.23	+0.10	–0.39
Nebraska	+1.81	+0.17	–0.10	+0.58	–0.10	+0.49
New Mexico	–0.27	–0.91	–1.22	–0.65	–0.80	–1.03
Oklahoma	+0.10	–0.40	–0.97	+0.70	0.00	–0.57
South Dakota	+0.38	+0.10	+0.74	+0.82	–0.10	+1.01
Texas	–0.99	–1.77	–1.44	–0.98	–0.50	–1.49
Wyoming	+0.13	–0.78	+0.28	–0.24	+0.20	–0.15
Average	+0.56	–0.66	–0.49	+0.08	–0.20	–0.25

Table showing annual changes in the water table in different parts of the Ogallala aquifer (measured in feet)

Item 2

Pickens's plan

In state after state and in scores of foreign countries, the demands of industry, agriculture and a burgeoning population are chafing against a finite supply of freshwater and the neglected needs of enfeebled environments. After 4 years of drought, Texas is a leading example.

As Texas's metropolises grow, the search for municipal water has become expensive and intense. Local entrepreneur Pickens hopes to capitalise on this by tapping the groundwater of four panhandle counties and sending it by pipeline hundreds of miles to one of three Texas cities — El Paso, San Antonio or Dallas-Fort Worth. The 654-mile pipeline Pickens envisages for El Paso would cost $2.1 billion, but he believes he can amortise that with the high water fees the city would have to pay.

On 26 December 2000, the *New York Times* carried a story about the Southern California Metropolitan Water District's plan to buy 145 000 acre-feet of water per year from Cadiz, Inc., a private company, yet Pickens's plan is bigger and more audacious. Pickens says Dallas would have to pay $675 per acre-foot for the water, while El Paso, separated from the panhandle by a mountain range, would face a $1400 per acre-foot charge. By contrast, the Southern California deal sets an initial levy of $230 per acre-foot.

Water for Pickens's plan would come from the panhandle portion of the Ogallala aquifer. One of the largest underground repositories of water in the world, the Ogallala stretches from Texas to South Dakota and once held more water than Lake Huron. That was a century ago, before the advent of cheap electric pumps gave farmers the power to lift water hundreds of feet. Statistics on the Ogallala are unreliable, but here's one — the aquifer waters one-fifth of the nation's irrigated land. Here's another — in less than a decade from its peak in 1978, the area of agricultural land irrigated by the Ogallala fell by 20%, at least partly because of the Ogallala's depletion.

The Ogallala is not like rivers, lakes or even most other aquifers. It has no source of replenishment. It holds 'fossil water', sealed underground for hundreds of thousands of years. Once it's been used, it's gone forever. Now, as the Ogallala aquifer's water level continues to fall, Pickens is proposing to expand its use, which is at the moment chiefly agricultural, to include supplying large, distant cities.

He's anything but apologetic. 'These wild statements like "Pickens is going to dry up the Ogallala" and "It's going back to a dust bowl" and all that stuff are baloney', Pickens said. 'Hell, I'm not about to dry up the [Ogallala] reservoir. But I don't mind selling surplus water'. Alas, one man's surplus is another's unsustainable resource.

In most states, Pickens would not enjoy the right to buy and sell groundwater, but Texas is the heart of the heartland, where regulation is considered inconsistent with the God-given right to make money. It is the only state in the arid West that legally acknowledges the 'right of capture', by which landowners have title to the water beneath them. Surface water is another story — even in Texas, rivers and lakes are part of the state's realm.

(Adapted from: **http://www.cero.columbia.edu/1115/web/main/1115_bk_frameset.html**)

Item 3

US statistics

- By 2050, the US population is projected to have increased by nearly 130 million people. This is the equivalent of adding another four states the size of California.
- Americans eat 815 billion calories of food each day. That's roughly 200 billion more than necessary and the excess is enough to feed 80 million people.
- Americans throw out 200 000 tonnes of edible food daily.
- The average individual daily consumption of water is 159 gallons, while more than half the world's population lives on 25 gallons.
- 40% of the US population drink well water, much of which receives little or no treatment.

- 50% of the wetlands, 90% of the northwestern old-growth forests and 99% of the tall-grass prairie have been destroyed in the last 200 years.
- 80% of the corn and 95% of the oats grown are fed to livestock.
- 56% of available farmland is used for beef production.

Item 4

Beef farming

Beef farming in the High Plains region has the advantage of using land that cannot be used for other purposes. When properly managed it promotes biodiversity, contributes to wildlife habitat, and provides both different sources of farm income and a healthy food supply. The greatest environmental problems from corn and soyabeans for animal feed are:

- irrigation (corn)
- soil erosion (soyabeans)

In addition, corn has serious implications for water quality because it is a row crop with high external inputs. The most unsustainable part of beef production is in the feedlot phase when cattle are fattened to satisfy the American taste for large steaks (which are frequently low in quality). Feedlots require huge amounts of water, both for the feedlot itself and for the irrigated corn that is fed to the cattle. This water often comes from depletable aquifers.

Historically located near the source of rain-fed corn in Illinois, Iowa, Ohio, Tennessee and Kentucky, feedlots have grown bigger and have moved west to more arid areas of the country such as the High Plains, where the environmental impacts of large amounts of animal waste are less, but feed is more expensive to produce and transport. The incentives to grow corn in areas of feedlot concentration increase irrigation, upset fragile hydrologic cycles and deplete aquifers. Land is ploughed, water is mined for irrigated corn to feed the livestock, and large quantities of manure are concentrated in small areas. As the feedlots moved west, so the demand for groundwater increased. Packing plants that depend on cheap labour and grain-fed cattle also rely heavily on water.

Shrubby plants have taken over much of the old grassland areas. Having animals in these areas could maintain biodiversity, decrease the need for feed and increase the quality of beef produced. Different ethnic groups have different taste preferences; the preference for large steaks is not shared by Hispanic or black Americans.

Current research suggests that keeping cattle out of feedlots for as long as possible has great potential for enhancing ecosystems, as well as diversifying meat supply in the USA. Part of the defensiveness of the organised livestock producers (apart from the tendency to view themselves as victims of urban interests, particularly those of environmentalists) is because in the past, rangelands have been very poorly managed. However, there are possibilities for sound management and learning from practices implemented elsewhere, so that high-quality forage-beef could be produced. At the same time, there would be increased biodiversity and decreased soil erosion.

Item 5

Statistics for the Ogallala aquifer and High Plains region

- It is the largest groundwater system in North America.
- Its 3.3 billion acre-feet of fresh water would fill Lake Huron, with enough water remaining to fill one-fifth of Lake Ontario. (An acre-foot of groundwater is enough to cover an acre of land with 1 ft of water and is approximately 325 000 gallons.)
- If pumped over the USA, the aquifer would cover all 50 states with 1.5 ft of water.
- If completely drained, it would take more than 6000 years to refill.
- Over 170 000 wells pump water from the aquifer — one for every square mile.
- Over 50 000 of these wells are in northwest Texas.
- More than 90% of the water pumped is used to irrigate crops. Withdrawals equal 30% of the total groundwater used for irrigation in the US.
- From the 1940s to 1980, the aquifer's average water level dropped by nearly 10 ft a year.
- The aquifer is responsible for $20 billion a year in food and fibre production.
- Texas can produce 2 million more bales of cotton a year because of the aquifer.
- The Texas High Plains account for 34% of the state's total cropland and 69% of the total irrigated cropland.
- Cotton, wheat and grain sorghum are the most significant Texan crops in the region.
- The aquifer covers 35 000 square miles in Texas (11% of the state's land).
- The mean precipitation range for the Texas High Plains is 14–22 inches.
- The saturated thickness in the Texas region averages 112 ft, with a range of 3–500 ft.

Item 6

Drought

Drought is speeding up depletion of the Ogallala aquifer. Eight university scientists recently spent a week in western Kansas measuring the water levels of 500 wells that draw water from the aquifer. They discovered that the water level is dropping faster than it did in the last decade.

'What happens when it gets dry, people pump more, so they're drawing on it more', said Rex Buchanan, Associate Director of the Kansas Geological Survey. 'These numbers clearly show the issue of depletion of the Ogallala is out there, and it's as pressing as, or more pressing than, it has been'.

(Adapted from: *US Water News Online*)

Resource-based question

(a) Describe and explain the changes to the Ogallala aquifer in recent times. (10 marks)

(b) Examine how changing values and attitudes might affect the use of the aquifer. (10 marks)

(c) Assess the likely impact of the falling water table on:

(i) the economy of the USA (10 marks)

(ii) the environment of the region (10 marks)

(d) To what extent can the Ogallala aquifer be managed as a sustainable resource? (10 marks)

Total: 50 marks

Candidate A's answer to question 1

(a) The aquifer is being used up rapidly with rates of depletion reaching 10 ft a year between 1940 and 1980. The main reason for this is that we have developed better technology, allowing wells to go deeper into the ground. Water is pumped out using cheap electric pumps. Approximately 170 000 wells have been dug to irrigate the region and as much water is drawn out as is taken out of the River Colorado. This is used to grow food for the American people (e.g. cotton).

e There is some attempt to address the depletion, but no use is made of Item 1, which shows that since 1980 there has been significant variation in depletion rates from place to place; indeed, in some areas water levels have risen. The explanation is a little thin, with only the use of pumps and the need for food being identified, notwithstanding the mistake of using cotton as an example of food! Urban demand is omitted, as are the changes in agriculture in recent times. With modest description and explanation, this answer scores 5 marks out of 10.

(b) When people first explored the region it was thought to be unfit for cultivation, but as soon as wells were sunk, water was used quickly by farmers without giving much thought to the future. Some people still want to keep using it, like Pickens, who is going to sell water to cities in the region, such as El Paso. This could only happen in Texas, where it is legal to take out groundwater from the ground you own. In other states you cannot sell water like this, so values and attitudes vary from place to place.

e This answer only touches on changing values and attitudes in the last sentence. The Pickens material should have been explored in greater detail. The values associated with the use of the High Plains for cattle rearing covered in Item 4 offered a series of possible contrasts in attitudes that were not explored. This response scores 5 marks out of 10 for description.

(c) (i) The whole of America is dependent on the aquifer, because food production from the High Plains region is very important. Without the aquifer, there would be much money lost by farmers who would probably go out of business. These unemployed farmers would be an extra burden on the American government and there would be a negative multiplier effect as farmers moved away and local shops and services lost business. This has happened already in this region. It might also be necessary to spend a lot of money on bringing in water from other sources like Canada, which would be very expensive. Americans are very wasteful people and the impact of falling crop yields would be reduced if they became more environmentally sensitive. They consume 159 gallons of water a day, which is six times the world average.

e A few useful links are made here, particularly the point about the negative multiplier, but the answer is not developed at a national scale. The likely impact of rising food prices is ignored, as is the possibility of rising water prices in the cities. Therefore, the answer is incomplete and not fully developed and scores 6 marks out of 10.

(c) (ii) If the water table fell, there would be many changes in the environment. The most obvious thing would be loss of farmland, some of which would revert to desert and scrub. Desertification would be made worse by the droughts of recent years. When crops cannot be grown there is more bare ground, so soil erosion would take place and rivers would become more choked with sediment.

e There is something here about desertification, but the links are only weakly established. The reference to recent drought is not supported by further material from Item 6. Once again, there is no reference to Item 4. It is vital that all resources are used. They contain information that would help with the answers to these questions. This response scores 5 marks out of 10.

(d) Sustainability is when the present generation does not destroy the environment, so that future generations can also enjoy it. This is also called intergenerational equity. The present use of the Ogallala aquifer is certainly not sustainable. At current rates, the aquifer will be gone by the year 2045 and it would take 6000 years to refill. Therefore, it is essential to cut water usage from the aquifer and not to allow the taking of water for drinking, as in the plan to sell water to the cities. Changes in farming practice would also help make the aquifer last longer. If Americans gave up their preferences for large steaks, and were prepared to eat less meat, then farmers would not need to fatten up cattle so much in feedlots. This would reduce water consumption. Better still, Americans could reduce their intake of burgers and steaks, which would not only make them healthier, but would also help protect the environment in places such as the High Plains.

e This response is a good example of a mid-range response, which identifies a number of issues, but fails to explore them. Thus, intergenerational equity is mentioned, but not explained. The problem is that the candidate does not recognise that the aquifer is not a renewable resource and will be depleted eventually, albeit at a rate to be determined by current usage. It is not 'preservable' in the sense implied here. This answer scores 6 marks out of 10.

e **Overall, Candidate A scores 27 marks out of 50.**

■ ■ ■

Candidate B's answer to question 1

(a) The Ogallala aquifer has been depleted a great deal since its discovery in the last century. It is predicted that at current rates it might be used up by 2045. However, in recent years the rate of depletion seems to have slowed down, although the recent drought seems to have speeded it up once more, at least in Kansas. The rate of depletion varies a great deal from place to place and some areas have shown an increase in water level in recent years. A century ago, the introduction of cheap electric pumps allowed the water to be used for agriculture for the first time, turning an area 'unfit for cultivation' into productive land. The changes in the level of the aquifer have come about as settlement has moved westwards and water usage has increased. The original use was for ranching. However, in recent years farming has become more intensive with the introduction of feedlots, which use large quantities of water. It is also predicted that the population of the US will increase by 130 million, placing further demands on well water supplies.

> This is a very capable response that covers most of the possible points. There could be more use of evidence from Item 1 — for example, stating where the water levels have risen. The explanation is good, although the last sentence is a view of the future rather than present use of the aquifer. This answer is awarded 9 marks out of 10.

(b) The most obvious sign of changing values and attitudes is that of selling the water from the aquifer in Texas, to cities. Pickens proposes to build a pipeline for $2.1 billion to serve El Paso or other cities. If this is allowed, it shows a change in attitude towards the aquifer, which, up until now, has largely been used for farming. There have also been changes in the American diet that have increased the demand for wheat, which if they changed back again would place less strain on the aquifer. The US wastes huge quantities of food; a less wasteful society would consume less and aquifer deletion would be reduced.

> Much of the material in Item 2 has not been used in this response. The attitude to groundwater varies from state to state, and only in Texas is the 'right of capture' acknowledged legally. This should have been explored, as should the points about consumption in Item 3, with a little more detail quoted. This response gains 7 marks out of 10.

(c) (i) The rural economy of the High Plains is almost totally dependent on the aquifer, which will inevitably run out one day. This region produces large quantities of food for the US and any decline in output would have a major impact on the economy. At present, it produces $20 billion worth of food and fibre. In Texas alone, 2 million extra bales of cotton are produced by using the aquifer. Food prices are bound to rise and US exports of wheat and grain would fall. As a result of the decline in farm income, all other incomes would also be reduced as the negative multiplier kicks in. Lack of local water supply would also mean that cities in the region would have to import water from other areas, at great expense. This would make everything more expensive and less competitive. Businesses located in arid regions might then choose to relocate to areas with cheaper water, which could be outside the USA altogether.

> This is a strong response, despite some reluctance to broaden out 'local' impacts to the whole country. Links are established between resources, although it would have been more sensible to quote source material more precisely as in 'as Item 4 shows...', thus drawing attention to the connections made. There is some additional applied understanding shown here with regard to the negative multiplier effect and relocation principles. The knowledge about the importance of

US exports is not explicitly rewarded, as it is not a specification requirement to have studied the USA. This answer is awarded full marks.

(c) (ii) The High Plains region has been dominated by rangeland agriculture for many years. Ever since the buffalo were destroyed, this area has been largely dominated by cattle ranching. The loss of the aquifer would threaten this environment because very low rainfall (14–22 in) occurs here. In recent years, intensive feedlots have increased damage to the ecosystems, but loss of water availability might change this and cattle grazing on the ranges is thought to be good for biodiversity. Recent drought would have changed the environment whatever land use was there, and past management has been poor.

e This is a reasonably comprehensive answer. However, the central point has not been raised. The aquifer was out of reach before well and pump technology developed, so the grassland ecosystem existed more or less independently of the vast groundwater reserve. Thus the loss of the aquifer would not change the 'natural' ecosystem; on the contrary, by evicting agriculture the 'original' structure of the High Plains might very well be restored. This point was a high band criterion, along with comprehensive use of facts and figures from the resources. This response scores 7 marks out of 10.

(d) The Ogallala aquifer is a non-renewable resource. It was formed more than 100 000 years ago and is not being replenished. Therefore it cannot be sustained for the future. Any use of it is a net reduction in the groundwater, so the only way of sustaining it is not to use it at all, which would be foolish as it is there to be used. It isn't like soil, which can be regenerated by the addition of organic and inorganic nutrients. However slowly we use the resource, one day it will run out, so future generations will not be able to use it. Sustainability means being able to meet the needs of the present without affecting the ability of future generations to meet their own needs. Future generations won't be able to use the Ogallala aquifer, although they may develop technology that enables them to survive in these regions without needing groundwater, just as we can survive in Britain without using the coal that is in the ground.

e This is an intelligent response that takes a view. This view does not stick very closely to the resources offered, but the candidate has a case to make and does it effectively. The central point is very well made and the link with sustainability is sophisticated. This answer is awarded full marks.

e **Overall, Candidate B scores 43 marks out of 50.**

Physical environments I

Explain why contrasting physical environments attract different levels and types of human activity.

Total: 25 marks

■ ■ ■

Candidate's answer to question 2

People like to live in a pleasant environment with nice views, fresh air and, in general, a nice climate.

e This is a horrible opening line. 'Niceness' is a relative concept and highly subjective. A nice climate for clubbers in Ibiza is not the same as a nice climate for wet-rice farmers in southeast Asia. Don't use it unless you can develop the idea.

This explains why about 90% of the world's population live within 50 miles of the coast. Also, most people take their holidays on the coast as the views are nice and the climate mostly pleasant. Most prefer to travel to the Mediterranean where there is warm weather and little rain. Most of the world's population lives in the northern hemisphere, as that is where most of the land is. In cold climates, like the Antarctic, there is little or no human activity as the climate is too harsh for our liking. The same can be said for desert areas, although there is slightly more human activity as nomads live within the desert, travelling from oasis to oasis. More people would live there if the climate weren't so harsh and dry. Egypt is a desert, but people live there because there is a source of water from the Nile. People tend to live on a relief that is flat because it is easier to grow crops and build housing, so the population on mountains is low. Most people live on flat land near the sea or a river. The land near a river is fertile because rivers flood annually and when they flood they leave fertile land behind, so less fertiliser is needed. Most of the population live where they do because that's where the cities or towns were originally founded, maybe because there was a defensive advantage, like a hill or a bend in the river, or they were near a forest or food source or a water source, like a spring. Chester is on a bend in the river Dee and London was built near a fuel source (forest), a river for protection and water supply and a marsh for further protection. These made people feel safe from any invading force. Tourism is another reason certain physical environments attract human activity as beaches in warm, pleasant climates attract a lot of tourism, so towns and cities are set up next to them because jobs are available. A volcano will attract human activity because the soil produced from the volcano is very fertile and good for crop growing, e.g. Mount Etna, where there are now cities. The population knows that the volcano might erupt, but people are willing to take the risk and live there because of fertile land and jobs. There is also a large tourist industry near volcanoes as people want to see what a volcano looks like and the view from near the top is good, as it is so high up. In Los Angeles, people live in an area prone to earthquake disasters, but are willing to live there, even though there is that risk, because there are jobs and a good climate. In Japan, there is little flat land but what there is, is located on the coast. So all the cities and almost all the population are located on the coast, with few inland as the relief is too steep for building permanent housing or farming.

e This is a very poorly structured paragraph. It contains a range of examples of how physical environments can affect human activity but it is not systematically presented. It would be so much better if it were 'cut and pasted', with reflective comments added, and divided into shorter paragraphs. There is also a lack of depth and detail in the examples — cities are not named and no data are used.

In conclusion, most of the world's population and human activity take place near the coast, in a warm pleasant environment that has some rain, as this is where people feel most comfortable in the world.

e This is a very disappointing return to the opening line, in which statements are made without any evidence being offered to support them. Conclusions should not repeat previous ideas — no marks are given for repetition.

e **This is a Level 3 response, scoring 10 marks out of 25.**

Human activity in LEDCs

Critically examine the view that human activity in LEDCs has more impact on the physical environment than in MEDCs.

Total: 25 marks

■ ■ ■

Candidate's answer to question 3

Human activities can be defined in terms of many things, including industry, agriculture, tourism and settlement. These activities necessarily have some impact on the natural environment, as they interfere with the natural balance of the system.

e It would be helpful to offer a view of what exactly is meant by the 'natural environment' or, at least, to raise the difficulty of these categorisations.

LEDCs are defined as such because they have less developed economies and therefore less capital. In Iceland, a periglacial region, agriculture is difficult to sustain because of the harsh climate and lack of fertile soils. This means that settlements are concentrated in small towns, which are extremely dispersed. The Inuits rely on subsistence fishing, which has little negative impact on the environment. However, after the discovery of oil there and in Alaska, the physical environment has been directly affected. There are few restrictions on the oil being extracted and the pipeline has caused environmental damage, destroying wildlife and causing pollution because of regular oil spills.

e This is a very confused response, with Iceland being offered up as an example of an LEDC and the Inuit being translocated several thousand kilometres to the east. However, factual errors of this sort would not be so critical if there were a relevant point being made. The example does not help to identify differential impact in these areas.

Alaska is of course technically part of the USA — an MEDC, but the way of life is more like that in an LEDC. Area 104, which was designated a wildlife zone, has been encroached upon, reducing biodiversity.

e Once again it is not clear what point is being made. The issue of the LEDC in an MEDC could be very interesting but it is not developed here.

In Bangladesh, an LEDC, the Ganges river has been terribly polluted. The lack of money to provide proper sewage treatment has meant that the raw sewage is pumped into the river, killing fish and other wildlife. Also, because of its religious significance, many thousands of people bathe there, causing the spread of disease and also erosion to the riverbanks. Hard-engineering schemes to try to reduce the risk of the Ganges flooding have meant that the natural sediment, which replenished the delta, is being prevented from coming downstream. Instead, more sediment is coming down from the Himalayas, where there is deforestation, causing soil erosion and deposition further upstream. This increases the risk of flooding in some areas.

e This screams out for further development. Is this evidence that the statement is more or less correct because such pollution is unknown in MEDCs, or is it just offered up in the hope that the relevance is self-evident?

More direct intervention has taken place in the Rhine in Germany. Industry used to dump chemicals and effluent, causing eutrophication and damage to fish and other wildlife. However, Germany, being an MEDC and a member of the EU, has sufficient capital to reduce pollution, unlike Bangladesh. Germany also has the ability to enforce laws, such as emission reductions for factories, whereas LEDCs don't have the capital or manpower.

e There is a point here. A case is being made that available capital limits damage by enabling anti-pollution laws to be enforced.

In Amazonia, the indigenous population of the Yanomani tribe practised 'slash and burn' agriculture in the rainforest. At this time, however, being an LEDC made little difference because the Yanomani were farming at a subsistence level and they had enough land for the soil nutrients to be replenished. However, there was a temporal change once commercial loggers started to reduce the size of the Yanomani's land. This resulted in soil degradation and erosion.

e There is a missed opportunity here to make the high-level comment that such logging is justified, by some people, by the pressure to provide foreign exchange or as a consequence of TNC operations that brings profits to MEDC-based companies.

In the UK, despite being an MEDC, there are spatial variations in the impact of agriculture. In Scotland, hill farming is the major form of agriculture, which, so long as the farmers don't overgraze the land, retains mostly the natural equilibrium. East Anglia is the most intensively farmed region in the UK. Huge amounts of herbicides and fertilisers, which can cause eutrophication, are used. Yet there are much tighter regulations on the use of chemicals in the UK than there are in LEDCs, so the impact on the environment is limited.

e This response has merit, but would be so much better if some comment had been made about intensive agriculture in LEDCs for the production of crops for export to MEDCs.

MEDCs are probably more aware of the impact of human activities on the physical environment because they have the money to research and investigate. LEDCs, however, despite knowing the consequences, may still decide to harm the environment because of a greater incentive, such as furthering economic development or improving the quality of life.

Japan intentionally did not have strict environmental regulations for industry post-1945, because it was desperate to become developed, whatever the costs. However, now the country is developed, it can try to rectify some of the damage caused. Impact on the environment can of course be unintentional, or indirect. The erosion of coastal defences down the coast from Dawlish Warren in Dorset prevented the movement of sediment to replenish its beach.

e The change of direction here is bewildering and, once again, the example is discarded without comment. The idea that values and attitudes have changed in Japan is sophisticated, but it needs 'flagging up' and making relevant to the title. What point is being made?

Human activities can, of course, have a positive environmental effect. The advent of ecotourism in LEDCs has led to the improvement of some areas by, for example, forestation. Australia's reefs are also being protected by ecotourism. The reversion to organic farming prevents build-up of dangerous chemicals. This is being encouraged, particularly among UK farmers.

However, the inappropriate use of MEDC technology in LEDCs is a significant problem. Prestige schemes, such as the Pergau Dam in Malaysia, require MEDC equipment and skills and since the LEDCs don't have the same level of government regulation, problems can occur. Similarly, chemical fertilisers in India are used without proper precautions, causing environmental damage.

Therefore, human activities do impact on LEDCs more than on MEDCs, but the MEDCs are also responsible for some of the problems. Until environmental concern becomes the top priority for all countries, the degradation will continue.

e The conclusion is weak, but the essay as a whole is stronger. It offers a wide range of evidence and is largely relevant. There is little critical examination in that, when a view is taken, it is stated rather than argued.

e **This essay is a good example of a low Level 4 response, scoring 16 marks out of 25.**

Physical environments II

Assess the view that the physical environment has to be managed if it is to be sustainable.

Total: 25 marks

Candidate's answer to question 4

The physical environment is a natural resource and unless it is used sustainably it will be ruined. This is why governments must protect it from being destroyed. There is increasing pressure put on the physical environment, as there is an increasing population. This is why overpopulation must not be allowed to occur. Examples of where sustainable development has been attempted are in the areas of tourism and opencast coal mining, and an example of where it has not occurred is in Uzebekistan.

e This is a series of bold assertions without any attempt to identify the key themes in the title, not least 'management' and 'sustainability'. This is a controversial topic and that does not emerge here. It would be better to establish what the essay is about by deconstructing the question.

Tourism has severely affected the Lake District. Twelve million people visit every year. This has damaged the physical environment through footpath erosion, litter, unsightly cafes, car parks and caravan parks. The National Park Authority has tried to keep restrictions on the total population and cap it at 40 000. Also, £500 000 has been spent on the repair of footpaths and areas have been sectioned off to stop hikers from damaging the landscape any further. At the present level of restrictions, the Lake District is being managed sustainably.

e The evidence here is good, with impressive detail, but the point is not explored fully. It would be so much stronger if some clues were offered about:

- how management is helping sustainability
- what sustainable management of the region actually means

Another example of sustainable development is tourism in Manaus, near the Amazon. This is called ecotourism. There is a 25 person lodge with no air conditioning, no hot water, solar power and the waste taken away in containers. This is sustainable because it is expensive and inaccessible. Also, the buildings look natural and blend in with the rainforest surroundings.

In South Wales there is a great deal of opencast coal mining. This process involves degradation of the physical environment and ruins the natural landscape. The local people don't agree with this and complain about it. As a result, the government has introduced a plan to re-landscape after mining has finished and to try to cause as little harm as possible. This has been done by using computer-aided design. Unfortunately, the attempts have not been successful and the landscape has not been restored. This is not sustainable development.

e This is all rather ambivalent and it is not clear what point is being made. Both examples are left hanging in mid-air. Do they tend to support the statement made in the question or not?

An example where sustainable development didn't happen to any extent was the Aral Sea in Uzebekistan. Farmers planted cotton, a cash crop, in semi-desert land. Cotton is a very thirsty crop, needing water. The government developed an expensive and inefficient irrigation scheme. The water used came from the Aral Sea and as it was free, the farmers used it extensively. They also made extensive use of fertilisers and pesticides. As a result, the sea level fell and the water supply was saturated. This occurred because the physical environment was used without respect, resulting in an environmental disaster.

In conclusion, this shows that if things are done with no regard for the physical environment, problems will occur. Also, with increased government intervention there will be an increase in the amount of sustainable development.

e The conclusion is unhelpful because, once again, the concept of sustainability is left unexplored. It is vital that key terms used in titles are defined. In this essay, the focus should have been the debate between those who believe that the physical environment has to be managed and those who believe that market forces will ensure that, as the costs of physical resources rise, demand will fall. This answer offers some case-study examples of the management of the physical environment, but there is no attempt to assess, and virtually no attempt to examine, management.

e **This is a Level 3 response, scoring 14 marks out 25.**

Question 5

Population movement

Examine the methods by which governments attempt to control population movement.

Total: 25 marks

■ ■ ■

Candidate's answer to question 5

Governments have attempted to control the number and distribution of people by regulating migration, commuting and tourism. These factors include direct and indirect policies that affect the distribution of people. Governments want to control the movement of people because it is inefficient to have regional variation. For example, in southeast England there are very high house prices and problems of traffic congestion, whereas in cities such as Liverpool and Sheffield de-industrialisation has left urban deprivation, unemployment and social unrest.

e This is a competent opening which addresses some of the basic causes of population policies to control movement, although there is no obvious evidence that the question has been properly deconstructed. For example, it would be useful to break up the local and national government policies.

Local authorities have attempted to build 100 000 new homes in Essex in order to distribute people within the southeast. New roads such as the M25 have been built to increase trade and influence people to commute rather than to move. The building of the A130 from Southend to Chelmsford has helped make these areas more accessible. The London fringe zone has also been increased. This is a zone in which doctors, nurses and teachers work within London, where they receive extra wages. It has been proposed to increase it to Brentwood. This is to encourage people to live in rural areas, and encourage suburbanisation. Not all such policies are specifically intended to control population movement, but may be more to do with relieving pressure in overcrowded regions or cities.

e There is reasonable detail here, but the response doesn't follow on logically from the opening. The focus on the title is not explicit, but there is a reflective comment at the end of the paragraph that makes it clear what point is being made.

In recent times, a charge of £5 has been introduced for bringing vehicles into London. This should encourage fewer people to commute by car and it might discourage the recent rapid growth of the London region. Commuting is a form of population movement. Park-and-ride schemes have also been introduced, for example in Cambridge. Local Councils have attempted to encourage movement to Southend with the use of the Internet, displaying Southend's attractions. Any improvement in the infrastructure will have this impact, because it affects the time taken and therefore the cost of journeys. The building of the channel tunnel, which involved huge expenditure by government, made southeast England even more attractive to inward investment and thus encouraged further population growth. After years of decline, in the last 10 years the population of London has increased by 500 000.

Once again this is a sensible answer. It lacks a precise point but includes the statement that 'commuting is a form of population movement', which helps focus on the question.

In many LEDCs, national governments have attempted to control the number and distribution of people. Sometimes this has been caused by a particular political approach. The creation of 'homelands' in South Africa is one of the best-known examples. The black population was forced to live in areas such as the Transkei, which had the poorest soils and the worst infrastructure. This was an attempt by the white minority government to create geographically distinct areas and was itself a development of the Group Areas Act of the 1950s, which divided up cities into racial districts. Mass migrations were not always enforced in this way. In India, after the partition of the separate Muslim state of Pakistan, a huge migration took place in both directions as Hindus and Muslims moved to India and Pakistan respectively. In Brazil, the capital was moved from Rio de Janeiro to Brasilia. This was to reduce population pressure in the southeast (48% of migrants a year migrate here) and to encourage economic growth in the central west. To encourage people to migrate here, employment opportunities were increased as TNCs were offered incentives. From 1991–96, 150 000 fewer people migrated away from Brasilia and only 2.7 million people migrated to the southeast, compared with 3.5 million people between 1986 and 1991. The government also built a road between Rio de Janeiro and Bari to encourage people to move away from Rio and commute. This was due to the increasing population pressure affecting economic growth in Rio, choking development through congestion and increasing land prices.

This is an exceptionally well-informed section of the essay. It is not flawless, but it is very impressive for an A-level student working under pressure.

Forest has also been cut down in the Amazon to encourage people to move to the northwest and start farming the land there. This is to reduce population pressure on the northeast where the land has been over-farmed, leading to soil degradation, erosion and loss of fertility. Some of this has been actively encouraged by government, with land grants to help prevent too much urban growth in São Paulo. Peasants have moved from southern states, such as Rio Grande do Sol, to equatorial states, such as Rondônia.

Between 1974 and 1988 in Indonesia, the government hoped to control the numbers of people living in Java by moving 1.5 million people to surrounding, less populated islands. This was done when Java reached its carrying capacity. Farmers were offered land as incentives to move and help distribute wealth. It was hoped that this would modernise farming, changing it from subsistent to commercial. This was to be done over a 3–5 year period. However, it caused much conflict among the local population. Such grand plans are particularly hard to carry out in democracies.

In the UK, the government has tried to revive population growth in economically depressed areas, for example south Wales. The Swansea enterprise zone tried to increase employment opportunities by building five commercial parks. The London docklands development scheme also tried to encourage urbanisation by changing industry from primary to quaternary, for example by building Canary Wharf and the setting up of the *Financial Times* offices.

e This paragraph is odd, because it returns to earlier themes and ideas.

This encouraged people to move back here, because of increased employment opportunities. In conclusion, the control depends on the development.

e After such an impressive review of the topic, this is a very disappointing finish. If the penultimate paragraph had tied it together, rather than repeating earlier ideas, this would have earned full marks. However, it lacks that final summative comment that is one of the criteria for the highest level.

e **This is a Level 5 response, scoring 23 marks out of 25.**